FRANÇOIS MANDEVILLE · TH

EDITED AND TRANSLATED BY RON SCOLLON

François Mandeville driving a dog wagon, possibly at Fort Smith, circa 1912

François Mandeville

This Is What They Say

A Story Cycle dictated in northern Alberta in 1928, edited and translated from Chipewyan by

Ron Scollon

Foreword by Robert Bringhurst

ᐯᑕᐠᐢᐊᐧ ᒪᐠᑌᐱᔆ

ᐁᐢᓂ

DOUGLAS & MCINTYRE · *D&M Publishers Inc. · Vancouver / Toronto*
UNIVERSITY OF WASHINGTON PRESS · *Seattle*

❡ Douglas & McIntyre
A division of D&M Publishers Inc.
2323 Quebec Street, Suite 201 · Vancouver BC
Canada V5T 4S7 *www.dmpibooks.com*

❡ Published in the United States of America by University of Washington Press
PO Box 50096 · Seattle, WA 98145-5096 USA
www.washington.edu/uwpress

Originated by Douglas & McIntyre.

Douglas & McIntyre gratefully acknowledges the financial support of the Canada Council for the Arts, the British Columbia Arts Council, the Province of British Columbia through the Book Publishing Tax Credit and the Government of Canada through the Book Publishing Industry Development Program (BPIDP) for our publishing activities.

The photo on the cover and frontispiece was formerly in the collection of Fr Louis Ménez, OMI (1922–2006), who arrived at Fort Resolution in 1949 and met François Mandeville shortly before the latter's death. This image was originally published in *Our Metis Heritage,* edited by Joanne Overvold (Metis Association of the Northwest Territories, 1976). The photo of the barren-land caribou on page 18 is from Creative Commons/Brian-0918. The photo on page 196 is from the Royal Alberta Museum, H73.55.1. The photo on page 198 is from the National Archives of Canada, PA-042083. The photo on page 224 is from the Glenbow Museum, NA-2617-46, and was identified by Philip Mandeville in 1976 as a photograph of his father. The photos on page 226 were taken by Ron Scollon.

The text face is Arno, designed by Robert Slimbach; the Canadian syllabic face is Euphemia, designed by William Ross Mills; the titling face is Cartier Book, designed by Carl Dair and revised by Rod McDonald. The sanserif is Scala Sans, designed by Martin Majoor.

Edited & designed by Robert Bringhurst. Printed and bound in Canada by Friesens. Printed on acid-free paper that is forest friendly (100% post-consumer recycled paper) and has been processed chlorine free.

· ·

Library and Archives Canada Cataloguing in Publication

Mandeville, François, 1878–1952
    This is what they say: stories / François Mandeville; editor, Robert Bringhurst; translator, Ronald Thomas Scollon.

Translated from the Chipewyan.
Includes bibliographical references.
ISBN 978-1-55365-473-5

    1. Chipewyan mythology.
    2. Chipewyan Indians – Folklore.
    3. Chipewyan Indians – Social life and customs.
    I. Bringhurst, Robert, 1946–
    II. Scollon, Ronald   III. Title.

E99.C59M35 2009   398.089'972
C2009-900905-6

· ·

Library of Congress Cataloging-in-Publication Data

Mandeville, François.
    This is what they say: a story cycle dictated in northern Alberta in 1928 / by François Mandeville; edited and translated from Chipewyan by Ron Scollon; foreword by Robert Bringhurst. – 1st ed.
       p. cm.
    Includes bibliographical references.
    ISBN 978-0-295-98933-4 (pbk. : alk. paper)
    1. Chipewyan Indians – Alberta – Folklore.
    2. Tales – Alberta.   3. Legends – Alberta.
    4. Folklore – Alberta.
    I. Scollon, Ronald, 1939–   II. Title.

E99.C59M35 2010
398.2097123—dc22   2009008563

Contents

CONTENTS

Foreword

t'a ?ánáwɛ́díi-t'á bịnikɛ́tc'a ?al'ị-hit'á
dɛne-ts'en hodeni-híłɛ ?ahot'ịį́
?ɛyi tθ'i hodɛlyụ́ų́ bɛnałɛ́ ?ɛkwáhodi.

He is told that if he handles game in a way
that goes against the mind of the animal,
it is unlucky for people.

This book is the joint work of three extraordinary people. They came together in two stages, half a century apart, in a twofold stroke of luck, and they took their luck to heart, collaborating earnestly and closely across three generations. At the core of their book is the voice of the eldest of the three: a very articulate Métis Canadian, sharing what he knew by telling stories he had listened to, thought about, and thought *with* all his life.

The storyteller, François Mandeville, was born on the shore of Great Slave Lake in 1878, spent his entire life in northern Canada, and died on the shore of Lake Athabasca in 1952. To city dwellers, this may sound like a spare and lonely existence, but to Mandeville it was otherwise. He knew and loved his world, and he had plenty of people to talk to – not least because he was fluent in every language, both indigenous and colonial, that was spoken in the region. Li Fang-kuei (or Lǐ Fāngguì), who wrote the stories down as Mandeville dictated them, in the Chipewyan language, was born in Guangzhou in 1902. He studied and taught for eight decades in Beijing, Ann Arbor, Chicago, Berlin, Honolulu, Seattle, and Taipei, and died in California in 1987. Ron Scollon, who lived and worked with Mandeville's stories for more than thirty years, and who twice translated them into English, was born in Detroit in 1939. He lived a life at least as peripatetic as Li's and died in Seattle on New Year's Day, 2009.

Mandeville passed the treasure of these stories on to Li in spoken form in 1928; Li handed them in manuscript to Scollon in 1973; Scollon took them back to share with Mandeville's descendants in Alberta in

1976 and now has handed them to us. Mandeville and Scollon never met, but over the years a bond grew up between them made of a great deal more than nouns, verbs, and phonemic notations on paper. In the form in which these stories come to us, there are three hearts beating in every sentence, three sharp minds thinking through the meaning of each phrase.

Native North American literature is a subject that has been trivialized and neglected over the past several centuries by almost everyone except aboriginal North Americans themselves and a few devoted specialists, like Li and Scollon, from outside. Many poets and novelists who lived in North America and wrote in English or French during Mandeville's time have found their way by now into the big encyclopedias, the literary histories, the schoolbooks and popular anthologies that help so much to spread their legacy around. Indigenous mythtellers, storytellers, and poets speaking or (in a few cases) writing in Native North American languages during the same period have been treated quite differently. The cultural machinery of North America, which is lubricated by advertising and built to handle salable commodities, like films, books, paintings, prints, theatrical events, and packaged performances, systematically ignores aboriginal oral literature and the mostly quiet, thoughtful artists who have made it what it is.

For hundreds of years, Native American oral poets and storytellers have done their work – and many are doing it still – in languages perched on the brink of extinction, but they have much to tell us all. Some of them are as brilliant and demanding as Wallace Stevens. Others, like Mandeville, are thoroughly down to earth. Many were and are understandably suspicious of outsiders, but many nevertheless, when offered the chance, have chosen to dictate their works to professional linguists, precisely in the hope that they might reach a wider audience, in a future which no one could clearly foresee. Such works survive in a hundred languages, as important as English, Spanish, and French to the torn, patched, and nonetheless still sumptuous fabric of North American literature.

Chipewyan, the language in which Mandeville dictated these stories, belongs to the Athabaskan family, a language group with more than forty members split into three major geographical areas. More than half these languages, including Chipewyan, are spoken in the Western Subarctic and Plateau: that is to say, the inland regions of Alaska, the Yukon, the western Northwest Territories, and much of British Columbia, Alberta, and Saskatchewan. Another eight Athabaskan languages – Hupa, Kato, Wailaki, and others – are spoken, or used to be spoken, in small pockets along the Cascades, in western Washington, Oregon, and California. Six more are spoken in the American Southwest. People with any interest in Native American life tend to know at least the names of some of those Southwestern Athabaskan languages: Navajo, Western Apache, and Chiricahua/Mescalero, for example. I do not know whether Mandeville ever heard any tales of his distant and older contemporary the Chiricahua warrior Goyaałé – known to most non-Athabaskans as Geronimo – but if these two men had met, they would have heard many familiar patterns in one another's speech and many familiar narrative structures in one another's stories. Chipewyan and Chiricahua are as close to each other as Spanish is to French, and speakers of both languages can therefore trace their history back to an ancient Athabaskan homeland, situated somewhere near the border of Alaska and the Yukon.

There are splendid works of literature recorded in Athabaskan languages from all three areas – the Subarctic, the Cascades, and the Southwest – and the range of literary styles, genres, and subject matter is wide. Someday, I hope, someone will write a good and thorough study of comparative Athabaskan oral literature, placing François Mandeville in the company of Navajo mythtellers such as Cháálatsoh (Charlie Mitchell) and Hastiin Hataałí (Singer Man), Chiricahua storytellers such as Sam Kenoi and Lawrence Mithlo, the Kato mythteller Hlonái kwe Kiileich (Bill Ray), and the great Koyukon storyteller Catherine Attla, a living example, born in 1927 in central Alaska.

In the modern university, First Nations literature has at long last become a respectable subject. It is, however, all too often taught with the unspoken requirement that, to make things easy for student and teacher, all the texts must be written in English. The syllabus then rapidly fills up with modern novels, composed by writers who live in the modern world but can claim some hereditary connection to one or several Native American groups. The implication is clear (though no one would be so uncouth as to speak it aloud) that race, not knowledge, is what matters. Beneath this lies another equally flawed and unstated presumption, that written English is a comfortably transparent and universal medium, imposing no cultural orientation or framework of its own. Mandeville is a wonderful reminder that the truth is more complex. He never left northern Canada, but when asked his nationality, he replied that he was French. He wore thick, Harry-Potter-style spectacles and European clothes, read the Bible, and professed the Roman Catholic faith. Even to Li, the perfect outsider (free, that is, of both colonial and missionary baggage), he would not tell any Chipewyan stories of the origin of the world. Yet his tales of hunters and animals are Athabaskan metaphysics incarnate. He achieved, with the Chipewyan language, the kind of symbiotic relationship that literature demands. He knew not just the meanings of the words, the permutations of the verb, and the syntax of the sentence. He had learned the motivic form of those much larger units of Chipewyan thought that we call stories. This made it possible for Mandeville and the stories to speak through one another, and that is what they did. What's more, since Li transcribed them in the original, that symbiotic speaking continues to resonate even now. The refined and attentive form of listening called *translation* can continue on and on.

Readers who want to consult a detailed map before embarking on the stories might turn first to Part III, "The Narrative Ethnography of François Mandeville" (page 227). In that very informative essay, Scollon explains how Li and Mandeville met, how the stories were transcribed, what kinds of things get lost when the Chipewyan sentences are translated into English, and why the oral versions are presented as they are on the printed page. He also deals with two important and unanswerable questions: *Who was François Mandeville?* and *Who was Li Fang-kuei?* It falls to me now to address briefly a third, no less unanswerable question: *Who was Ron Scollon?*

Ron was a linguist but never satisfied with studying language alone. He understood the nuclear physics of words and sentences as well as anyone else, but he was far more interested in how speech functions in its context when humans interact with one another and the world. And so with his wife, Suzanne Wong Scollon, he pioneered a field that he and others liked to call "the ethnography of speaking." In his twenties he studied Spanish, Japanese, and Korean, as well as the important and much-neglected language of music. In his early thirties he began to work on Mandarin, Cantonese, and Gwich'in, an Athabaskan language that is spoken all across the northern Yukon and in adjacent parts of Alaska and the Northwest Territories. On the heels of that experience came his seminal encounter with Li Fang-kuei in Honolulu, and then with Li's transcriptions of Mandeville's stories. He earned a Ph.D. in linguistics from the University of Hawai'i at the age of 34, then taught in Honolulu, Fairbanks, Taiwan, Seoul, Vancouver, Victoria, Hong Kong, and at Georgetown University in Washington, D.C. He was at ease in the academy but never quite found room there for his spirit or his vision of the field in which he worked. So while he published more than a dozen books with academic presses and close to a hundred articles in academic journals, he was always reaching out beyond those bounds.

His first book, an outgrowth of his doctoral dissertation, was called *Conversations with a One-Year-Old.* Then there were papers with titles like "The Rhythmic Integration of Ordinary Talk," "Fast English, Slow Food, and Intercultural Exchanges," and "Metaphors of Conflict from Gilgamesh to Saddam Hussein." He analyzed the differing roles that knocking and coughing played in Asian and American conversation, examined the interrelations of conversation and physical work, and raised a lot of pointed questions, including: "Will Pac-Man gobble up the humanities?" and "Can mediated discourse analysis stop the war?"

When he went to Fort Chipewyan, Alberta, in 1976, to meet the descendants of François Mandeville and to get acquainted with Mandeville's world, he also set up a Native Studies program for students at the local school. When he joined the University of Alaska, he also got involved with the Alaska Humanities Forum and soon became its chairman. He sat on the editorial boards of at least half a dozen scholarly journals, served as advisory editor to a similar number of university presses, and later became consulting expert on intercultural communication to the United Nations Institute for Disarmament Research. In Alaska in the mid-1980s, he also founded two exemplary anti-institutional institutions, the Axe Handle Academy and the Gutenberg Dump. The latter was an old-fashioned intellectual midden for recycling good used ideas. The mandate of the former was essentially the same but more specific, therefore more complex. Gary Snyder described it as "an imaginary university of proto-humanism"; Scollon called it "a school for making schools" and "a school of ecological arts."

The Axe Handle plan was to integrate local and imported knowledge by training teachers and students alike, all across Alaska, to find their way in the global village by reference to an actual home place. This involved bioregional studies – learning what lives where, how it lives, what it needs in order to continue, and what human beings need to do to coexist with all that other life. It also involved an ambitious curriculum of literary classics – Native American as well as European, Asian, African, and Oceanic. Alaskan students would therefore learn to read – and Alaskan teachers would learn to teach – Tlingit, Haida, Eyak, Aleut, Yupik, Alutiiq, Iñupiaq, and northern Athabaskan literary classics alongside Sophocles, Lao Zi, Dante, Shakespeare, Goethe, and whatever else seemed good enough to flourish in this company. There was no reason, of course, why the academy should confine itself to Alaska; that was merely a convenient place to start. So is everywhere else. And this is one more book that belongs on the Axe Handle bookshelf.

In the last year of his life, Ron knew that he was dying and that nothing could be done about it. He met this knowledge with extraordinary grace, eager to live all the life he had left. What he wanted to do most, along with visiting a few friends and relatives, and spending time with the woman and the children he loved most, was to return to Mandeville's stories. He'd translated them first in the 1970s. He was keen to have another go at showing how they worked. He thought he could translate them in a way that might elucidate just how un-English and un-European they are, and at the same time show how intercultural communication works, in literature as well as face to face, if it's given a fair chance.

Communication is never passive. Mandeville, Li, and Scollon have each done their part. It is up to us as readers to do the rest.

— ROBERT BRINGHURST
Juneau · 27 March 2009

Translator's Preface

François Mandeville was a storyteller, an avid reader, and a writer. It is not known whether any writing in his own hand remains. He told this set of stories to Li Fang-kuei in the six weeks centering on July of the summer of 1928. Philip Xavier Mandeville, his son, said that François Mandeville knew many more stories than are recorded here. This is a selection François Mandeville himself made from his much larger repertoire. Mandeville chose a core group of sixteen stories as a way of guiding Li Fang-kuei in his understanding of the Chipewyan people. They constitute a narrative ethnography.

In one case – the story "His Grandmother Raised Him" – Mandeville deferred to his elder, Baptiste Forcier. He also told five additional stories which are accounts of activities from making a canoe to tanning a moose hide – topics which were suggested by Li Fang-kuei. While these stories lie outside the central set of narratives, they too shed light not only on Mandeville's own life but on how he understood the lives of the people about whom he was telling these stories.

Neither 'narrative' nor 'ethnography' is Mandeville's term. It is unlikely that he would have known either word. Perhaps he would have been surprised to see his stories translated and presented in this light. They are also not terms used by Li Fang-kuei.

I have called these stories a narrative ethnography because in this collaborative project Mandeville has given us a quite comprehensive view of how Indians teach, how wolves teach, how humans are to live with wolves, how we are to live with bears, how canoes are made and hides tanned. We learn how the Dené made the extremely important discoveries of copper and iron. We learn of the human and sometimes complex, even hostile relationships among the people who in English have most often been called Chipewyan, Slavey, Yellowknives, Inuit, Dogribs, Hare, Métis, and French.

The territory covered in these stories ranges from Fort Chipewyan at the west end of Lake Athabasca to Fond du Lac at the eastern end, and from that lake northward to the barren lands and the Arctic Ocean.

Here we learn of different kinds of special powers – 'dreaming' (in a pair of stories about the Wise Man), 'medicine' (in the four-part story of Raven Head and in "The Adventures of Beaulieu") and 'capability' (in "Education"). We learn that those who are truly capable prefer to hide their strengths (in the story of Scabby) and to favor those who discover these strengths and respect them without antagonism or rancor ("His Grandmother Raised Him").

I have edited this book to honor the two men who produced this collaboration, François Mandeville (1878–1952) and Li Fang-kuei (1902–1987). They met in the summer of 1928 and worked together for just six weeks of very intensive linguistic-ethnological storytelling and analysis. To see this collaboration from the point of view of Professor Li, in the way I did as his student for a number of years, is to see it as one of the most densely concentrated periods of fieldwork in Athabaskan linguistics or perhaps in any linguistic fieldwork project. In those six weeks, Li collected ten notebooks of dictated stories and 2,800 file slips densely filled with verb paradigms and other lexical notes. Li made at least one file slip for every word in each of the twenty-one stories.

But seeing this work as merely a collection of texts for linguistic analysis now seems to me far too narrow a view of the collaboration between the two men. Mandeville was also working on his own project, certainly as hard as Professor Li, during these same six weeks. In 1977 at Fort Smith, Northwest Territories, his son, P. X. Mandeville, told me that his father had for many years tried to develop his own writing system to overcome the inadequacies of using English or French alphabets, or Cree syllabics and their corresponding pronunciations to write the First Nations languages in which he was competent. These languages included Chipewyan, Slavey, Dogrib, Hare, Gwich'in (Loucheux) or, as his son put it, 'all the languages down the [Mackenzie] River.' When Li met him and asked him to dictate stories, Mandeville saw his chance and, according to his son, spent his evenings after intensive days of work with Li practicing the writing he was watching Li do during the day. At the time I spoke with him, Philip did not know whether any of his father's writing had survived the almost fifty years since their collaboration. Thus the only record we have of that collaboration is the meticulous notes Li prepared.

Mandeville was an interpreter among many other things, following in the footsteps of his own father, Michel Mandeville, who was an interpreter-translator for the Treaty Eight Commission in 1899. Mandeville himself often worked as a court interpreter. His son suggested to me that his father had always wanted to 'write about the Chipewyan people.' It was apparently for this reason he worked so assiduously at learning Li's orthography for the language. But while he was studying the orthography in preparation, I believe he was also laying out what amounts to a narrative ethnography of the Chipewyan people in the stories he told.

All of the stories he told to Li are here in this book. This translation began with the transcription and translation of the stories we published as Li & Scollon 1976. While that translation was of some use for linguistic purposes, it was not as useful for those who want to read Mandeville's stories. In this translation I have reanalyzed the Chipewyan stories from the point of view of narrative structure as developed by Jacobs (1959), Hymes (1981), and Tedlock (1972a, b), and in a few of my own publications. I have also returned in every case to Li's original 1928 phonetic transcriptions and field notes to reconsider clause and sentence structures in seeking to arrive at a translation which would be both accurate and readable for a reader with no knowledge of Chipewyan.

In addition to the stories themselves, I have included an essay of my own which may, for some readers, enhance the understanding of these stories and the history of the collaboration of Mandeville and Li. The appendix gives facsimile examples of several of the stages through which these stories have passed from the original dictations in 1928 to the present edition.

All of Li Fang-kuei's original materials on which this book is based are located in the Fanggui Li Collection of the American Philosophical Society, Philadelphia. I wish to thank Laurence C. Thompson and Terry Thompson for their support of Li Fang-kuei in the first place, then of my own work with Professor Li's Chipewyan materials, and finally for making sure they were archived safely for posterity when Professor Li would no longer be able to use them. I have greatly benefited over the years from discussions and sometimes arguments with Dell and Virginia Hymes. This work would not exist without their continued insistence that stories such as these of François Mandeville belong among the great expressions of the human spirit. Discussions with Dennis Tedlock helped me to see how to bring together both the analysis of written transcriptions made from dictations such as these and of transcriptions from recordings which preserve the voice of the storyteller.

This is a project I have wanted to work on since finishing the first translation three decades ago. I might never have come around to doing it were it not for the encouragement of Robert Bringhurst, who prodded me until I could think of no further excuses not to get started.

Richard Dauenhauer and Nora Marks Dauenhauer have been inspirations in so many ways it would be impossible to enumerate them here. Their lifetime work of bringing the classics of Tlingit literature to publication is not matched anywhere in the world. It has been a pleasure for these three decades and now more to be able to continue to talk with them about their work and ours, trying to get straight how we can do the work of getting such stories out into public view while keeping ourselves from seeking to academically upstage the storytellers themselves.

Finally, although this particular project is my own, from our first meeting in Whitehorse, Yukon, four decades ago I have enjoyed learning together with my wife and colleague, Suzie Wong Scollon, what Athabaskan people have to tell us about our lives and how to live them. It is the rarest of wives who can succeed in getting her husband to sometimes just shut up and listen.

— RON SCOLLON

Part One: The Stories

1 How Copper Was Discovered

[PROLOGUE]

Long ago the people fought the barren-land enemy.

Then again they fought.

Then when the barren-land enemy had killed all of the people

> only one woman survived.
> They took her with them
> when they returned to their land.

They made the woman keep her head covered with a tanned hide.

> One of the enemy led her by holding her hand.

> Every day they traveled in that way with the woman.
> This is what they say.

When they stopped to sleep at night

> they bound the woman's feet together.
> They also tied her hands.

> Then they covered the woman with a musk ox hide.
> One of them lay down along the edge on each side.

> They were afraid that she might suddenly escape during the night.

> That's how they watched her.
> This is what they say.

[ACT I, SCENE I]

When the barren-land enemy got home they said,

> "This woman should be killed."

Usually when they bring a person they have captured home
they make a big feast and dance.

While they're dancing they bring the stranger in there.
All of them dance in turn.
Whoever is dancing holds a knife while he is dancing.

He cuts a small piece of flesh from that stranger with the knife.

He eats it.
When he has done that,
another takes his place.

That one also cuts out a piece of that stranger's flesh
and he eats it.

They do that to the stranger, cutting out little pieces of flesh.

They do it until the captive dies.
When the barren-ground enemy captures strangers
and takes them home,
this is how they kill them.

[ACT I, SCENE II]

Well, they brought the woman in.

They all said,

"Let's kill her like we always do."

Now before a captive is killed,
they take the captive to the chief to see.

He looks the captive over carefully.

If he says the captive should be killed,
they kill him.

If he says not to kill him,
then he is not killed.

[ACT I, SCENE III]

That was their custom and so they now brought the woman in.

They made her go before the chief.

The chief examined her very carefully.

For a long time he did not speak.

Well, some of the young men there said,

"Hurry up!
We want fresh human blood.
Let's dance!"

But the chief didn't say anything yet.

[ACT I, SCENE IV]

Suddenly he spoke out after a long silence.

"Don't kill this woman.
This woman is still a girl.
She's beautiful,
and I also think she'd be a good worker.
We'll make her one of our relatives."

So they didn't kill the woman,
but the chief made her marry one of his sons.

That's how the woman ended up staying with them.

The woman wanted to go to her own land
but she didn't know which direction to go.
She didn't know where they'd come to
because the hide had been covering her head.

[ACT II, SCENE I]

She stayed with the barren-ground enemy for a long time
until she had a child.

She carried the child,
who was beginning to talk a little,
around with her wherever she went.

She went quite a distance from her home
down to the edge of the ocean.

There was a long point extending out into the sea.
When she got close to that point
she suddenly saw a caribou
going out along that point.

The woman got up on a rock and sat.

From there she watched the caribou.
When the caribou came to the end of the point
it just went right on out into the ocean.

And so, going on, it disappeared.

After that another caribou came.

Again it did the same.
It disappeared out toward where no land could be seen.

The woman wondered,

"How can that be?
There is no ground you can see.
But the caribou aren't swimming
because it looks like their legs are walking.
The water there can't be very deep.
The ground must go right across underneath.

"Could the caribou go across the ocean like that?"

So she started over where they were going.

She was thinking,

"I'll give this a good look."

When she got there
she saw the caribou trail was deeply worn into the ground.

It went along the point and right out into the water.

So that's where she went.
From there she looked out onto the sea.
She saw that the ground extended out under the water.
Also from place to place the ground appeared to rise
    out of the water.

Now while she was standing there, another caribou started out.

She watched it carefully.

> As it moved out into the water,
> the water didn't come above its feet,
> even as far out as she could no longer see its legs.
> Gradually the whole body disappeared in the distance.

Well, now she thought about it.

> "The caribou are walking across the ocean,
>   but they don't come back.
>   There is no land I can see in that direction
>   so there must be land lying right underneath the surface.
>   I'll follow the caribou.
>
> "If I die, I am not with my relatives anyway.
>   Dying among the barren-land enemy
>   or dying alone are all the same to me."

[ACT II, SCENE II]

So that was it. She went after the caribou,
carrying her baby on her back.

She walked on the land
that lay just below the surface of the water.

> From time to time the land rose up above the water,
> and she walked on that.
> Again near the end there was no land.
> But she walked on the ground underneath the water.

She was able to travel quickly like that.

Suddenly she thought,

> "If the enemy came after me,
>   they'd catch up with me."

So she traveled on day and night.

There was only one place where it was deep,
just up to her belt.
She waded through there.

And so she walked.
No land could be seen all around her.

Then all of a sudden something came into sight behind her.
She thought,

    "It must be the enemy coming behind me."

So she hurried on as quickly as she could.

[ACT II, SCENE III]

Before she had gone much farther, she saw land.

    She walked in that direction.

Whatever she had seen behind her was coming closer.

    But she couldn't see what it was.

    As she got close to the land
she could see what was coming behind her.
As it got closer,
she could see a lot of caribou were running toward her.

[ACT II, SCENE IV]

Well, just at the same time that the caribou reached her,
she came to the land.

Coming to the land, she jumped off to one side.

    The caribou all came out of the water onto land,
following the caribou trail.

[ACT III, SCENE I]

Now she didn't have any idea what land she had come to.

Even though she was on the land now,
she went on a long way.
She didn't make camp
and she didn't eat.

So she became exhausted.

[ACT III, SCENE II]

Finally she came to a good place with good moss.

She unpacked her child
and lay down on the moss.

She slept for a long time before she woke up.

Then she was very hungry,
but she had no meat to eat.

[ACT III, SCENE III]

Now the caribou were coming up on land one right after the other.

The line extended out as far as the eye could see.

She thought,

"I wonder how I can kill a caribou?"

So she got her awl from inside her awl bag.

Then she looked along the shore.

She found a stick more than twice her height,
and she tied her awl to the end of that.
Then she sat down
by the place where the caribou were coming out.

The caribou kept coming past her.

When she saw a good fat one
she killed it by spearing it.

She pulled it over to one side of the trail.

All she had was a small knife,
but she cut up the caribou with that.

She cut some of the meat into very thin pieces.

She dried them by spreading them out on a rock.

[ACT III, SCENE IV]

In order to make a fire, she gathered a lot of dry moss together.

Then she went to look for pieces of quartz.

She put two pieces of quartz down
on the dry moss she had gathered.
She struck them together.
The sparks from the rocks fell on the dry moss,
and it caught fire.

Once she had built up the fire, she roasted some meat.

She ate that with her child.

[ACT IV, SCENE I]

Well, then the child began to talk to his mother
like people talk to their wives.

He said,

"Wife!"

He didn't mean well by it,
so she just sat there.

She thought,

"I'd better leave him behind."

So she put a hot stone inside the caribou stomach
and cooked the blood.

When the blood was cooked,
she lay the child down inside the stomach.

Then she told him,

    "My boy,
      wait here for me and eat.
      I'm going to get some berries.
      Sit here until I get back."

    And so she left him.

[ACT IV, SCENE II]

But then she suddenly thought,

    "What if he starts to follow me?"

    So she climbed up a hill
    and looked back from there.

She saw he was still sitting in the stomach, using his hand to eat.

[ACT IV, SCENE III]

Then she really left.

    She didn't know which direction her land was,
    so she went toward the sun at noon.

    That's how she traveled.

[ACT IV, SCENE IV]

When evening came, she lay down.

    Early the next morning she started off again
    even before the sun came up.

She had gone a long way when night fell.

    She saw reflected light up under the sky
    in the direction she was going.

    At first she thought,

"There must be a big fire burning up ahead."

She kept on going
since she was already traveling in that direction.

Many nights passed and she could see
that the light in the sky was getting brighter.

But the light was there only at night.
It couldn't be seen in the daylight.
So she traveled that way only at night.

[ACT IV, SCENE V]

When she got to that place, the light in the sky disappeared.

She stood there among whatever it was
the light was coming out of.
But she didn't have any idea what it was.

It looked like meat from a lot of game animals,
cut up and spread out to dry.

She picked up a piece of it, thinking,

"What is this?
I'll take a good look at it."

It was heavy,
and it looked a lot like meat, but it wasn't meat.
It was heavier than meat.

She walked all around among it.

It looked like a lot of game had been cut up.
Some of it looked like hide,
some of it like dry meat,
but also ribs and backbone meat.
It had all the shapes of pieces of game.

That's what it was like.
They just were lying there.

Well, the woman thought,

"This isn't of any use to me.
      But if I happen to see some people while I'm still alive
      I'll have them look at it."

So she took a small piece of it and started off again.

She went off in the same direction she had been traveling.

[ACT V, SCENE I]

Well, after she had gone a long way
she came across some people.

   She discovered that the people spoke the same language she did.

   So she told those people all about what she had done:
   how the people had fought,
   and also how she had stayed with the barren-land enemy.
   She told about how she had walked across the sea
   and that she had seen something
   which was like meat but wasn't meat.

   She told them everything about that.

   Then she also showed them the piece of it
   she had brought with her

[ACT V, SCENE II]

Well, they said,

      "This could be useful.
        Let's go find it."

So she started off to find it again,
taking the people with her.

[ACT V, SCENE III]

When they came to it they picked up some of it.

   The woman told them,

"We don't know what this is.
   Be sure to take good care of it.
   Also be sure not to do wicked things here on the earth."

But while they were staying there,
a man behaved badly with her.
He used his body to harm her.
The woman tried to fight him off,
but he overpowered her and did as he wanted to do.

The woman became very angry,
and the others all wanted to leave there.
This is what they say.

   She said,

   "I'm not going to leave here."

And she just sat.

They said that they wouldn't go without her.
This is what they say.

They tried to carry her off,
but they couldn't lift her.
This is what they say.

So they started away from there.
This is what they say.

[EPILOGUE]

After a long time the people came to that place again.

They found the woman still sitting
in the same place she had been sitting.

   Her body had sunk about halfway down into the ground.
   But she didn't speak to the people.

And the copper that was lying there
had gone halfway into the ground.
This is what they say.

Again, long after that they went there again.

> Now they found that only the woman's hair could be seen.
> The copper had also all gone under the ground.
> Nearly all of it was out of sight now.
> Only parts of some of it could be seen.

> They gathered up whatever they could
> from the little they could see.
> This is what they say.

Yet again, a very long time afterward they went back to it.

> Nothing could be seen.
> The woman had gone under the ground.
> Also all of the copper had disappeared with her.
> They had to search under the ground to find it.

> That's the only way they could find it.
> This is what they say.

> Finally, because it went so far underground
> and was so difficult to get,
> they abandoned it.
> This is what they say.

Li 1928: 1.37–11.15 / Li & Scollon 1976: 28–59

2 How Iron Was Discovered

There was a man named Beaver Orphan.

He had strong powers and he could do anything.
This is what they say.

Because of this, people followed him wherever he went.

[SCENE I]

Once, he started out again to the barren land.

Many people were traveling with him in that direction.

Finally he had gone a long way.

There in the barren land one of the men said to him,

"We have come a long way into the land of the Eskimos.
It wouldn't be good to come across them suddenly.
We have so many children with us,
if we started to fight,
many of the children would be killed.
But you have led us all this way into their land."

But Beaver Orphan didn't say anything.

He just continued farther on.
This is what they say.

[SCENE II]

After a long time they came to the shore of the ocean.

They went down to the beach.
There they saw a place where many caribou had passed.

So they camped right there
and soon they had killed many caribou.

[SCENE III]

Then one day one of the young men who'd been out hunting

came back and said,

> "I was walking along the beach
> and came across something,
> but I don't know what it was.
> It looked a lot like stone,
> but it wasn't stone.
> It was a lot like wood,
> but it wasn't wood either."

One of the people questioned him,

> "Was that thing you're talking about heavy?"

He answered,

> "I don't know.
> I didn't touch it."

[SCENE IV]

So the next day they said,

> "Let's go where that thing is.
> Let's have a look at it.
> Maybe somebody knows what it is."

So that day they went off.

They found it,
but nobody knew what it was.

They just came home and told Beaver Orphan.

He said,

> "I want to see that thing you're talking about too."

[SCENE V]

They started out the next morning,
Beaver Orphan going along with the people.

But he didn't know what it was either.

Well, they didn't know what to do.

One of the boys hit it with a stone.
It just rang but it didn't move.
They couldn't even see a mark
where he'd hit it with the stone.

Finally a lot of the boys hit it with stones.
It just rang.

They still didn't know what the thing was.

They said,

"Let's try burning it."

So they made a fire over it.

The thing became red in the fire,
but it didn't burn up.

Then as the fire went out,
the thing just went back to looking the way it had before.

[SCENE VI]

Then Beaver Orphan told them,

"I had a dream about something.
This seems to be what I dreamed about.
I'll try to think about it."

So he sat down on the end of it and began to sing.

He sang for a while.

Then he took it in his hand
and lifted it right up.

34

He carried it around over his head with one hand.
Even though it was heavy, it wasn't heavy for him.

Then he said,

> "This is what I dreamed about.
> This is it.
> I was told that it is called iron.
> Now I found what it is.
>
> "Now I was told that this thing is very useful.
> Maybe it's hopeless but I'll try it again."

And he began to sing again.

[SCENE VII]

After he had sung a little he took it by one end.

He put that end close to his mouth.
Then as he was singing, he blew on it.

It broke in half, ringing.

He blew it again.

Again it rang and broke apart.
It split apart like it was wood.

He put the pieces down separately.

Then taking a piece,
he did the same thing again.
He blew it again
and he broke it apart.

He broke them all apart in small pieces like wood.
This is what they say.

[SCENE VIII]

So they distributed all that iron among themselves.

They made arrowheads with it.

They also made spears.
That's what they did with it.

[EPILOGUE]

So they got a lot of use out of it.
This is what they say.

    That's how iron was first discovered.
    This is what they say.

Li 1928: 11.16–27 / Li & Scollon 1976: 60–69

3 Raven Head

[PROLOGUE]

In the summer many people were camped together.

Raven Head was living there with them.

They decided to form a war party.
This what they say.

Raven Head went with them.

Now in the summer when they go on a raid,

    someone makes them small birch cups to drink water.
    Each of them has one tied on so he can drink.
    When they're on a raid
    they don't drink water lying down on their chests.
    That's too dangerous.
    This is what they say.

[ACT I, SCENE I]

Raven Head's younger sister made a birchbark cup for him.

    He had it tied on,
    but whenever they drank water, he said,

      "Lend me a cup so I can drink."

He said this every time.

Finally one of them wondered,

      "Why does he say that?
      He has a cup,
      but whenever we drink water, he says,

'Lend me a cup.'"

Raven Head answered him,

"I can't drink from my cup.
  My sister's making fun of me."

He didn't say anything else.

[ACT I, SCENE II]

They were traveling on.

Yet again when they drank water, he said,

"Lend me a cup."

They told him,

"Drink from your own cup
  We're not going to lend you a cup."

He answered again,

"I can't drink water from this cup.
  My sister is making fun of me."

But he didn't explain anything further about it.

That's how they went to war.

[ACT I, SCENE III]

When they had traveled a long way,
        they came upon the Dogribs' camp.

They set up not very far away from there.
Their plan was to charge them first thing in the morning at dawn.
So they waited close by all night.

[ACT I, SCENE IV]

At daybreak they charged.

They rushed at them along the lake.

When they were still only about halfway along
    the distance of the lake,
they could see Raven Head was already up ahead
    on the land above the Dogribs.

He soon disappeared among the Dogrib people.

No sooner had he disappeared among them
than Dogribs began to yell.
Nobody could tell what they were saying.
Wherever he went among them, they were yelling.

When the yelling finally came to where the tepees were set up,

    the shouting stopped.

Then they heard Raven Head shouting out,

    "That's all.
      The last is sticking up without a leg."

So they went to join him there.

Even though he hadn't killed a single Dogrib
he had broken all of their left legs and their right arms with a club.

That's how they were when the people got there.

They killed all of the Dogribs after Raven Head
    had first wounded them.

Once all the Dogribs were dead,
they gathered up anything that might be useful.

Then they started away from there.

    [ACT II, SCENE I]

They were still going away from home when autumn passed.

Then when everything was frozen they started back home.

They were heavily loaded with the things
they had taken from the Dogribs they had killed.
They couldn't move very fast.

39

They weren't going along all together.
Each went along a good distance after the other.
Some of them went in groups of three people
or four or five of them.

That's how they were going home.

[ACT II, SCENE II]

Then when Raven Head wasn't around, some of them said,

"Why is it that when we fight,
   people can't kill anyone before him?
We need to find out what's going on.
When he comes to us,
   we'll race up to those two people
   who are walking on the lake ahead of us.
We'll tell him they're enemies."

So they waited until Raven Head came along.

[ACT II, SCENE III]

When Raven Head came up to them, they said,

"Raven Head,
   why is it that you always club our enemies to death
      before anybody else?
We want to find out what's going on.

"Let's race to those two people over there on the lake.
We'll see who will get there first."

At once Raven Head said,

"Sure,"

and they took off running toward those two men.

Before they had run even halfway to them,
Raven Head sped past, leaving the men behind.
The snow was flying up from his snowshoes,
making a tail in the air behind him.

When he caught up with the first one,
he stabbed him in the middle of his back.
Then he stabbed the other one.
The two men collapsed to one side of the trail,
with blood streaming out of their throats.

Then he turned back
to the people coming behind and yelled,

"The last one is sticking up without a leg."

So they came to him.

The two people he had killed were lying there.
Nothing could be done about them now.
So they got furious with Raven Head.
They complained to him,

"You are not like a human being.
You've just killed our own relatives."

Raven Head answered,

"You're the ones who said
that we'd suppose they were our enemy
and race to them.
You said to do what we would do if they were the enemy,
so that's what I've done – just like they were the enemy.
I killed them.
If you hadn't told me that, I wouldn't have done it."

[ACT II, SCENE IV]

Well, the dead men's relatives were really sorry about that.

Even while they were still crying, they said to Raven Head,

"Bring these men back to life.
You've got powers which you can use to kill people.
It shouldn't be very hard for you to bring them back to life."

But Raven Head answered,

"You don't kill things so that when they're dead

you can bring them back to life.
If I kill somebody,
it's because I want them to be dead.
I don't want to bring them back to life after that."

[ACT II, SCENE V]

They couldn't sit there doing nothing
        because they had to keep traveling.

The two men were already dead,
so nothing could be done about that.

So after sitting there alongside of them crying only for a while,
they started off again.

They said to Raven Head,

    "Come with us."

But he answered,

    "You're already mad at me.
    I don't want to travel with you."

So they left while he was still just sitting there.

So they traveled again.

[ACT II, SCENE VI]

They traveled all day long.

When the sun was nearly set,
they heard people talking on the trail behind them.
But they couldn't see anyone who might be talking.
They could only see Raven Head back there.

They wondered,

    "Who could he be talking with?
    Let's wait here for him and see."

Then suddenly they came out of the woods.
There were three of them,
and Raven Head was walking between the other two men.

The two men Raven Head had killed
were walking alongside on each side of him,
and there was nothing wrong with them.
He was going along saying funny things,
and the two men were having a good laugh together with him.

That's how they came up to the people.
This is what they say.

Everybody was happy that their dead relatives had come back okay.

[ACT III, SCENE I]

Well, they say that since the time they'd left home,
Raven Head hadn't eaten anything.

There was no meat because they had found no caribou.
Raven Head said,

"I'll go ahead of you again.
You follow my trail.
I'm going to get home ahead of you."

When he'd said that he started off.

Nobody could say anything against him.

They were too frightened of him,
because he wasn't like other people.

So they followed on the trail he had left.

They came across a small clearing in the woods
full of his tracks all around.
His tracks went all over, crossing each other in all directions.
When they came to that they wondered,

"What has Raven Head done here to make so many tracks?"

43

When they examined the tracks closely
they saw places between his tracks
where the snow hadn't been touched.
In those places they saw some weasel tracks.
Otherwise there were no other tracks.

Then they found that he had started off again from there.

So they set out again following his tracks.

Going along that way in the woods,
the ones who were ahead started running back, shouting,

"There's a big bear!"

And they all turned and ran.

But then one of them said,

"There's no point in running.
Let's try to kill it with spears.
We'll just wait here for it.
When it comes,
we'll all spear it at once from both sides of the trail.
We should be able to kill it that way."

[ACT III, SCENE II]

So they set up their ambush.

They sat there waiting for a while,
but there was no bear.

One of them said,

"What's happening?
If a big bear sees something move,
he doesn't run away from it.
Maybe you people didn't see a bear after all."

But the person who'd seen the bear said,

"It's a big bear all right.
And it's not very far.

I walked up to it
close enough that I could see all of its teeth."

So they said,

"We'd better go take a look."

So then two men started ahead to see the bear.

Just like before they came running back terrified.
They came back, shouting,

"There's a big bear!"

But there was still no bear.

Well, this time they said,

"Maybe the bear killed Raven Head.
It doesn't want to leave his body.
Let's go see what's happening."

So they walked along to where it was.
They were walking along the trail through the brush.

Suddenly they came to a turn in the trail.
And there was the big bear standing up.
It was very close and its mouth was wide open.

But one of the brave ones looked carefully.
He saw that the bear's mouth was propped open with a stick.
He said,

"This bear isn't alive.
His mouth is open,
but he's not moving."

He watched it for a little while
but it didn't move,
so he went up to it.

When he got to it
he learned for certain that the bear was dead.
Everyone came up to it.

Raven Head had killed the bear with a horn club.

He'd smashed the jaw into two pieces,
but he'd cut out only the fat between its legs.
That was all he took from it.

He'd stood the bear up like that by the trail
and propped its mouth open with a stick.

That's what he'd done.
This is what they say.

[ACT III, SCENE III]

Raven Head had made a fire.

He put the fat from between the bear's legs on a stick.

He caught the dripping grease
with the cup he had said his sister made to make fun of him.

Then he set out again without eating anything.
This is what they say.

Well, the people were hungry so they cut up the bear.

They ate their fill of that meat.
Then they set out again, following Raven Head's tracks.

[ACT IV, SCENE I]

They were going against a cold west wind headed toward home.

They went out onto the lake which was near their houses.
They came onto it from the lower end
where the west wind drifts onto the shore.
There they could see something in the compacted snowdrift
        beside the trail.
A man's penis was sticking up out of the snowdrift.

One of them said,

    "What on earth is that?
    It looks like a man's penis.
    It's just sticking up out of the snowdrift."

All of a sudden Raven Head said,

> "It is a man's penis!
> It's my penis!"

There he was waiting for the people to come.

They told him, lying there in the snow,

> "Come on with us.
> Let's go home together."

But he said,

> "No.
> When you get there,
> tell my sister to come here where I am."

So everybody went home without him.

[ACT IV, SCENE II]

When they got home they said,

> "Raven Head wants his sister to go to him.
> He's lying over at the end of the lake in the snowdrift
> with his penis sticking out.
> He said to tell you."

Raven Head's mother and father said,

> "He just isn't like other people.
> We know he'll do something to his sister.
> We won't let her go to him."

But they said that Raven Head had said,

> "Don't stop her from coming to me.
> Tell them how I'm lying here."

Then the girl said,

> "I'm not going to go to my brother."

Her mother and father agreed.

So a man went back to Raven Head and told him.

"Your sister says she won't come here to you.
Your mother and father also agree."

Raven Head wasn't happy with this. He said,

"Hurry up!
My sister has to come here
and see my penis."

He said,

"My mother and father shouldn't say she can't do that.
Now hurry!"

So the man went back and told them.

[ACT IV, SCENE III]

Well, the old man got mad and said,

"Raven Head isn't like people.
His sister isn't going to go to him lying like that."

They told Raven Head again,
and yet again he got very angry.

Suddenly he got up.
He broke out of the frozen snowdrift
and started running to their home,
the snow flying up behind him in a tail.

When they saw Raven Head coming they said,

"Raven Head isn't like people.
He's going to do something to his sister,"

and they all piled up on top of her to hide her.

When Raven Head came in

he saw that his sister's foot was sticking out
from under the people lying on top of each other.

As soon as he saw that, he grabbed it.
He pulled on it.
There were so many people lying on top of her,
it was hard to pull her out.
So he tore her whole leg out.

He went outside and tossed her leg to one side in the snow.

Then he just went back to his own house.

[ACT IV, SCENE IV]

Just as he got home, his mother came after him, crying.

"Your sister is pitiful.
Bring this one you have killed back to life for me.
Your father and I are pitiful.
We only have your sister to work for us,
and now you've killed her."

But talking to Raven Head was not like talking to people.
His father came.
He said the same thing,
but Raven Head didn't say anything.

Later his father and mother came together to see him.

Again they pleaded with him.

Suddenly Raven Head got up.
He said,

"Go home, both of you!
That's enough!
I'm fed up with your noise."

He got up and went out.
His sister's leg was lying there frozen in the snow.
He grabbed it and went back to his father's house.

He went over to where his sister's corpse was lying.

He threw her leg at her and said,

"Get up!"

And immediately his sister sat up.

[ACT IV, SCENE V]

Raven Head turned to his father and his mother.

He told them,

"You say you love your daughter.
    That's what you say but you don't really love her.
    If you loved her you'd talk to her well.
    If you had told her how to be good,
    she wouldn't have made me a birchbark cup
        with her pubic hair.

"She just doesn't know how to be good,
    so she made a cup for me with her pubic hair.
    If it had not been me,
    if she had done that to someone else,
    and he drank water from that cup,
    it would have killed him instantly.

"If I hadn't seen that,
    it would have killed me.
    But I saw that she tried to kill me.
    So I didn't die from it.

"From now on she won't do that again to people
    or she herself will die.

"To prevent that,
    you'd better talk well to her
    if you love her."

And when he'd said that, he just walked out again.
This is what they say.

•••• *Part 2* ••••

[PROLOGUE]

People were camped one spring at a fishing lake.
This is what they say.

[ACT I, SCENE I]

Raven Head and his young brother went off to get birchbark
      for a canoe.

  They went a long way, but he didn't peel any bark.

  There was a lot of good birchbark, but he said,

    "This isn't good.
    There must be better birchbark farther on."

Finally many days passed.

Suddenly he said,

    "Let's peel birchbark here."

[ACT I, SCENE II]

When they finished peeling bark,
he said to his young brother,

      "Brother,
      we have been away from home for a long time.
      I worry that the enemy must have killed everybody.
      Let's hurry home."

That really scared his young brother.

  It seemed as if he already knew
      that the enemy had killed people in their absence.
  But he didn't say anything to him.

  So they started going home.

51

[ACT I, SCENE III]

They had come a long way away from home,
and so it was a long time before they arrived back.

They found out that everybody there had been killed.

Everywhere they went they found only dead people.
Raven Head walked around among all the bodies.

Suddenly he said,

"Brother,
the enemy were very happy here.
It looks like they killed everybody."

Then Raven Head searched among all of the dead people.

He found where his father and his mother were lying,
and brought them together.
Then he told his young brother,

"Brother,
I'm going to lie down here with my father and my mother.
Don't talk to me if it's just about nothing."

And he spread a raven skin blanket over himself
and lay down between his father and his mother.

He lay there for a long time without moving.

[ACT I, SCENE IV]

In time the bodies began to rot.

They were crawling with maggots.
Raven Head's raven skin blanket was also crawling with maggots.
But he himself did not move.

His young brother came to him.
He wondered if he was breathing
and so put his face close to him.
He didn't feel any breath.

Raven Head's brother stayed this way.

[ACT II, SCENE I]

Suddenly he saw a lot of sharp-pointed canoes
   on the lake approaching him.

He went to his elder brother and said,

   "Brother,
   the enemy is coming."

But Raven Head didn't move.

He told him again,
but still he didn't move.

The enemy was now getting very close.

The boy was terrified
because he was still very young.

He thought,

   "I guess the ghosts of our people have killed Raven Head.
   He doesn't move when I speak to him."

Then he thought,

   "It looks like the enemy will kill me now.
   I can't defend myself against them,"

and the boy started to cry.

Out of nowhere it suddenly occurred to the boy to say,

   "Raven Head,
   a wolverine is coming toward us!"

   "What?"

Raven Head threw off his raven skin blanket.
He jumped up and said,

   "What did you say?"

His brother pointed to all the people coming in canoes,

   "Look over there!
   It looks like wolverines."

53

Raven Head looked. He said,

"It looks like a lot of people."

Then he said,

"Brother,
let's get over there into the woods."

So they went into the woods.

He shook the decayed wood out of the center of a birch.

Then he told his brother,

"Brother,
stand inside of this.
Watch me from here."

And he cut a hole in the birch so he could see out.

[ACT II, SCENE II]

Raven Head went back to his blanket,
grabbed it, and headed for the shore.

When he got there he made himself into a small boy.

He just sat there.

Many people were coming in canoes.

They finally got there.

All of a sudden one of the Dogribs said,

"Ain't it around here we killed all them people?"

They all looked toward the land and they said,

"It was right here we killed them all.
Right here."

They all looked toward the shore.

Right then, just like a little child with a blanket on his back,
Raven Head started to crawl away from the shore.

They all said,

> "How come a little child is crawling around here?"

As they started to land they were saying,

> "What does he live on?
> Is he eating the corpses?"

One of the Dogribs said,

> "Let's not kill him right away.
> We'll have some fun first before we kill him."

And they all came ashore.
They said,

> "Let's play with him with little willow sticks."

[ACT II, SCENE III]

Raven Head pretended to be scared
and started to crawl away from them.

> When the Dogribs caught up to him
> they hit him with little willow sticks they threw,
> and they laughed at him

> Raven Head pretended to cry like a child
> and kept crawling away from them.

The Dogribs told him,

> "Hey kid,
> look at the sun.
> Right now you're seeing the sun for the last time.
> You're going to die right here."

And they kept throwing sticks at him.

> Raven Head kept kicking his legs,
> moving away from them,
> and crying.

In that way he gradually got quite a way away from the lake.
A lot of Dogribs followed him.

They kept tormenting him and laughing at him.

At last all of the canoes had come in to shore.

Raven Head kept watching
until the last one had come ashore.

When they were a long way from the lake
the Dogribs told Raven Head again,

"Kid,
we're not joking.
Look at the sun.
Look at it for the last time before you die."

[ACT II, SCENE IV]

Suddenly when they weren't paying attention,
Raven Head jumped up.

He tossed his raven skin blanket off to one side.

"You told me to look at the sun one last time.
I guess you won't be too happy looking at the sun now."

And he clubbed down the nearest two men with his horn club.

They all shouted and started running to their canoes.

"How can this be?
It looks like Raven Head."

But Raven Head ran between them and their canoes,
clubbing down all of the Dogribs
who had headed for their canoes.
Not even one Dogrib had brought a spear with him.
So they had nothing at all to defend themselves.

In that way he wounded all of the Dogribs.

Raven Head broke one arm and one leg of all of the Dogribs.

When the last one fell, he said,

"Okay, that's finished.
  The last one is sticking up without a leg."

He went back to his young brother.

He lifted up the decayed birch trunk,
and his brother came out from under it.
He said,

"Brother,
  these Dogribs killed our relatives.
  Now get a spear and go kill all of them."

So the boy got a spear from one of the Dogribs' canoes.

He went around spearing all of them.

The boy was going around among the wounded Dogribs,
    killing them.

The Dogribs made obscene gestures at him.

"Sure,
  you think you are a man.
  But you wouldn't be trying to act like a man
  if it was just you alone."

That's how they taunted the boy.

[ACT III, SCENE I]

Once the boy had killed all of the Dogribs, Raven Head said,

"Brother.

"Now you go make a canoe.
  I'm going to go wash off the maggot excrement.
  Tell me when you've got the canoe finished."

And he went into the water down at the shore.

His brother made a canoe.

He finally got it finished.

Then he also made two paddles.

At last after that he went down to the shore.

He called out,

"Brother!"

But there was no answer.

Again he called out,

"Brother!"

Yet again there was no answer.

Finally the boy started to think,

"My brother must have drowned,"

and he started to cry.

[ACT III, SCENE II]

He was going along the shore, crying,

"My brother."

Suddenly Raven Head emerged from the water and said,

"What do you want?
I'm just washing the maggot excrement off myself.
How come you're calling me now?"

The boy said,

"I've finished making the canoe.
That's why I've been calling you."

So Raven Head went to see the canoe.

Once he had examined it very carefully, he said,

"Okay, brother,
now we'll head up north."

But before they got into the canoe, Raven Head said,

"Brother,
  we've killed all these people.
  But it's best when you kill an enemy
  to take something from them.
  This what they say.

"Go cut off all the Dogribs' penises."

[ACT III, SCENE III]

After the boy had done that
he strung all the Dogribs' penises on a line.

He stretched the line all round the gunwale of the canoe.

  That's how they started off to the north.

[ACT III, SCENE IV]

They carried the canoe over all of the portages.

  That's how they canoed their way north.

But it was summer and getting hot.
All of the penises were starting to rot and to stink.
So the boy untied one
and pushed it into the water.

Raven Head saw that.
He said,

  "How come there's just a knot here?"

Finally they were really stinking,
so the boy pushed them into the water two or three at a time.

Raven Head saw that and again he said,

  "Here I've found another knot."

In that way the boy finally shoved them all into the water.

At last only the line was strung on the gunwale.
This is what they say.

[ACT IV, SCENE I]

Well, the boy was thinking about his relatives and his parents
who had been killed.

> Sometimes he cried because he was feeling lonesome.
> But Raven Head didn't say anything.

One evening the young man was crying again out of lonesomeness.

> Raven Head asked,

>> "Brother,
>> why are you crying?
>> Our relatives have speared caribou up north
>> at a caribou crossing.

>> "They are running around playing with a ball
>> where there are white tepees standing on flat sandy ground.

>> "I don't think they're crying over us."

> But he didn't say any more than that.

Then the boy thought,

>> "How can that be?
>> We left all our relatives dead back there."

> So they went on canoeing north.

[ACT IV, SCENE II]

They finally came to the lake with the caribou crossing.

> The sun had passed noon when they got there.
> They could see a lot of white tepees standing there.
> So they canoed right toward the tepees.

> When they had come near,
> the people who were staying there came down to the shore.

> Raven Head's father and mother saw a canoe,

and they had come close,
so they canoed out to see them.

They said,

> "Our sons went looking for birchbark back in early spring.
> Everybody said that they must have been killed over there.
> Now it looks like they've come here to us."

They said this as they paddled out to meet their two children.

Raven Head said,

> "The enemy can't kill me.
> I had thought that the enemy had only killed you."

[EPILOGUE]

If people have done no wrong, when they die

> they go to that place where Raven Head
>   and his younger brother canoed.
> This is what they say.

•••• *Part 3* ••••

[ACT I, SCENE I]

One of the people said,

> "Let's get up a war party without Raven Head.
> Whenever he's with us,
> no one else is able to kill the enemy.
> We only get to kill the enemy after he's wounded them.
> It's no fun to kill wounded people like that.
> Let's go without letting him know."

So they didn't tell Raven Head.

They spread news of their plan
to everybody who was staying there.
And they all separately started preparing to go on a raid.
They passed the word to each other and said,

> "Well go as soon as we've all gathered together."

So they all came together at the place they'd agreed.

They made one of them the leader
because he was known to have the strongest powers.

That's how they started out on a raid with their war party.

[ACT I, SCENE II]

They finally came to the land of the Dogribs.

But they didn't find any Dogribs.

The leader of the war party practiced his powers.
He looked ahead.
With his powers he saw where the Dogribs were staying.
Singing out with his powers, he told them.

So the next day they started to go in the direction
where he had said they'd find the Dogribs.

[ACT I, SCENE III]

In the evening just as the sun was nearly set,

    they came to a lake where the Dogribs were staying.

They sat down a little distance away from the Dogribs.

They planned to charge them first thing in the morning.

When dawn came, though, one person said,

    "Let's have a good look.
      There might be too many of them."

One of the men climbed a tree.

    From up there he looked at the Dogrib camp.

    "It looks to me like there are too many of them.
      I see a lot of fires."

But it still wasn't very light,
so they took turns climbing up the tree to look.
From up there they all looked at the Dogribs' camp.

[ACT I, SCENE IV]

All of a sudden someone spoke to them.

    "How come you're sitting up there?"

And Raven Head came out of the woods toward them.

They answered,

    "We thought there were fires over there.
      That's why we've been looking,
        but now there don't seem to be fires."

He stepped out of his snowshoes and said,

    "I want to have a look."

So he climbed up a big tree.

He got up where he could see the fires,
but he said,

> "I can't see very well from here."

And he climbed farther up.

They all said,

> "Raven Head,
>   it's already getting light.
>   The Dogribs will see you,
>   so don't climb up too far."

But Raven Head said,

> "I still can't see from here.
>   I want to get a good look."

And he kept climbing up higher.

[ACT I, SCENE V]

Well, one of them grabbed Raven Head's snowshoe.

> With his knife he cut it all up.
> He cut up all the webbing
> and he broke the frame into small pieces.

> Then he grabbed the other one.
> He did the same thing with that one.
> And then he scattered the pieces all over in the snow.

[ACT I, SCENE VI]

Then right away they charged the Dogribs.

> Raven Head started to climb down from the tree.
> He said,

> "It's all tied up in knots."

They had already started to run away from there on their raid.

When they were well out into the middle of the lake,
Raven Head sped past, leaving everybody behind.
His snowshoes were making the snow fly up behind him.

And so he came to the shore.
People were shouting all among the tepees .
His relatives didn't understand.

When they had nearly got to him, he said,

"Now the last is sticking up without a leg."

He had wounded all of the Dogribs.
They lay spread around here and there.
When the people got to him,
he was just standing there among them.

He said,

"I've made it easy for you.
You can kill them now."

So again Raven Head's relatives were mad at him.
One of them asked him,

"How come you have wounded them?
You kill them yourself.
We don't want to kill them."

Raven Head said,

"Right.
If you had been by yourselves
you'd never have been able to defend yourselves.
The Dogribs would have killed you.
That's why I've protected you.

"You said,

'We'll go kill Dogribs without him,'

and started out on this raid without me.
But here without me you would have all been killed.
You're still alive because I have defended you again.

Now you say you don't want to kill the wounded,
but you can't kill any who aren't wounded."

And when he'd said that he left to go home.

[ACT I, SCENE VII]

Well, Raven Head had known exactly
when they had left to go on their raid.

But he hadn't said anything to anybody.

He'd just stayed there at home.

Then suddenly he'd said,

"People have gone on a raid with a war party.
They might have been killed.
I'd better go after them if that's all there are."

That's how he had come to his relatives
just when they were going to charge the Dogribs.

That's what they had found out.
This is what they say.

[ACT II, SCENE I]

Sometime after that his relatives came home.

They were so angry they didn't bring anything
from the Dogribs they had killed.
This is what they say.

Raven Head told them,

"You've said that you haven't killed anybody by yourselves.
That's why you got mad.
From now on you can go on raids by yourselves.
You tell me that it's no fun to kill people I've already wounded.

"Well, now you can kill Dogribs who haven't been wounded.
I hope you enjoy yourselves."

[ACT II, SCENE II]

So his relatives decided to go out on another raid.

> Not even one of those who left on the raid ever returned.
> Apparently they were all killed by the Dogribs.
> This is what they say.

> Raven Head said,

>> "They went off on a raid, saying
>> they were going to enjoy killing Dogribs.
>> Maybe they killed a lot of Dogribs,
>> but they haven't come home for a long time.

>> "They were still alive because I defended them.
>> I told them that they'd be clubbed down like puppies
>> if they were by themselves.
>> I guess that's what happened."

> Well, those who had gone out on the raid never came back.
> This is what they say.

•••• *Part 4* ••••

[PROLOGUE]

Everything was easy for Raven Head.

[SCENE I]

Suddenly he found that he couldn't kill anything
when he was hunting.

He left the people, taking his wife and his children with him.

Even though he was hunting he didn't kill anything.

Only with the greatest of difficulty was he able to kill
something to eat.

Then they came upon a group of people camping.
So they stayed there with them.

[SCENE II]

From the time he joined those people,
they couldn't kill anything either.

So they all left that place.

Raven Head also went along with them.
The men went out hunting.
Every day until after the twilight became night,
Raven Head, his wife, and his children followed the people
on the lake.

[SCENE III]

Then a small fire showed up on the shore.

Nearby another small fire could be seen.
Then there was another fire a bit farther on.

Raven Head's daughter asked,

"Mother,
  that looks like a fire over there.
  What is it?"

She answered,

"No, daughter,
  it isn't anything."

Just standing there
they could see fires extending all round the lakeshore.

So the woman said to her child,

"Child,
  it's like a fire over there,
  but we don't know what it is.
  Don't tell your father about it."

And so they went on.

They came to the place where the people had made camp.

Raven Head returned
after she had finished making camp.

He hadn't killed anything to eat that day.

[SCENE IV]

One of his daughters asked,

"Father,
  we passed a lot of things like fires.
  What are those?"

No sooner had she said that
than he grabbed his horn club and rushed out.

As he was going out he said,

"I think this has something to do with my weakness in killing.
  Don't joke about it."

And he started running back on the trail to the lake.

Well, the woman got angry with her daughter.

She said,

> "I told you not to tell your father about that.
> We don't have any idea what it is.
> It might do something awful to your father."

[SCENE V]

Raven Head was still gone when dawn came.

The wife of Raven Head told all the people,

> "Last night my daughter told my husband
> that we saw many fires.
> He went back to those fires.
> He hasn't come back yet."

So the people started back to the lake.

[SCENE VI]

When they got to the lake
they saw where he had started to walk out on the lake.

> He had been clubbing the ice people.
> So they followed his tracks
> where he gone around clubbing the ice people.
> They followed his tracks all around the lake.

> Then they came upon Raven Head's dead body.
> This is what they say.

There was no blood anywhere,
and so they all examined it carefully.

They agreed,

> "We have to find out how he died."

So they all examined him.
But they didn't find any wound anywhere on him.

One of them was looking at his fingers.
He found a small splinter of ice under the fingernail
     on the little finger.
That was all they saw.
They couldn't see anything else.

[EPILOGUE]

It was his heart.

That ice splinter had stabbed it.

They found out that was how he was killed.
This is what they say.

This is a set of four distinct stories. They are grouped here as four parts in a single story as they were in the original dictation (Li 1928), where no titles were given following the first one. The originals can be located as follows by parts:

Part 1: Li 1928: II.28–III.19 / Li & Scollon 1976: 70–97
Part 2: Li 1928: III.19–50 / Li & Scollon 1976: 98–123
Part 3: Li 1928: III.51–IV.7 / Li & Scollon 1976: 124–135
Part 4: Li 1928: IV.7–15 / Li & Scollon 1976: 136–143

4 His Grandmother Raised Him

Told by Baptiste Forcier

[PROLOGUE]

Once, people were camped.

> An old woman who was raising her grandson
> stayed there along with the other people.

[SCENE I]

Her grandson became displeased with the people,

> and he said to his grandmother,
>
>> "Let's leave these people."
>>
>> "If we leave them, what will we eat?"
>
> His Grandmother Raised Him said,
>
>> "Don't worry about that; we'll probably live."
>
> And so they left the people.

[SCENE II]

Not too long after they had left,

> he said to his grandmother,
>
>> "Go around to the places where they make their fires.
>> Most likely they've already gone away.
>> If they're gone, gather all of their tentpoles together
>> and burn them all."
>
> She went and then came back to him.

He asked his grandmother,

"Have they left?
And did you gather all their tent poles together?"

His grandmother said,

"I have gathered them all up."

"Did you light fire to them?"

His grandmother said,

"Yes."

After that he sent his grandmother back
to check on how the poles had burned.

His grandmother went back,
because he wanted to know how the poles had burned.
She returned to him.
He asked his grandmother,

"How did the poles burn?"

"The poles in your uncles' camps burned into pointed shapes.
The others burned into round shapes."

"Those with the round shapes will starve to death."

Then he left her there.

[SCENE III]

He was gone for a long time before he returned.

His grandmother asked him,

"Where did you stay?
You were gone a long time."

"I was enjoying living with the caribou.
That's why I was away so long."

Then he untied his belt
and a lot of caribou tongues fell out.

That made his grandmother very happy,
and they ate up all the tongues.

Later in the evening he said to his grandmother,

"Let's go over there to see if they're dead."

[SCENE IV]

They left the next morning.

When they came to a lake,
they saw many dead caribou lying there.
His grandmother was really happy
because she saw lots of dead caribou.

She cut it all up.
They packed the meat together,
and then the old woman dried all of it.

So they set out after his uncles
and they lived well with all of that meat.

The other people didn't do well.
They all starved to death.

[EPILOGUE]

From then on His Grandmother Raised Him led the people,
and they enjoyed camping with the caribou.

Since that time the caribou have lived together with people.

Li 1928: III.1–7 / Li & Scollon 1976: not published.

The story was told to François Mandeville and Li Fang-kuei by Baptiste Forcier at Mandeville's invitation. Mandeville considered Forcier to be a superior storyteller. For a discussion of this complex issue, see pp 229, 237, 258–260.

5 Scabby

There was a boy whose body was covered with scabs.
This is what they say.

He was covered with scabs
       except for his face, his hands, and the soles of his feet.
This is what they say.

His parents took care of him.

    Still he got more scabs.
    If he moved, the scabs would crack and then bleed.

    Because of that his parents didn't want to take care of him.

    That's how he came to be staying with his grandmother.

So his grandmother cared for him.

    She made clothing out of rabbit skin for him.
    This is what they say.

    Wherever the people went,
    his grandmother carried him around after them.

[ACT I, SCENE I]

The sun returned and it became warm again where they were staying.

    All the children were playing outside,
    chasing and calling each other around the houses.

Scabby said,

    "Grandmother,
     put me outside.
     I want to watch the children playing."

His grandmother said,

> "Be quiet and sit.
> They've told you that they don't like to look at you.
> That's why you are staying here with me.
> Don't look at people."

But Scabby said,

> "Nobody will die if I look at them.
> Take me outside."

So finally his grandmother took him out.

She set him down by the door on one side.

His grandmother was doing some work.
It was a long way from their home.
So she left to go there.

That evening the children finished playing.

When the old woman came home
she brought Scabby inside.

[ACT I, SCENE II]

A wise man who was living there said,

> "I want all of the children to come to me.
> They must come in one by one."

He had them pass the word among all the houses,
and the children came to him.
He said,

> "Don't all come in at the same time.
> Only come in one at a time."

So one of the boys went in.

The wise man looked him over very carefully.

Then he said,

"Okay, Grandson,
    that's enough for you.

"You can go home again."

Then another one came in.
He told that one the same thing
and sent him home.

So all of the children had come to him and returned home.

[ACT I, SCENE III]

Only Scabby had not been seen by the wise man.

He told his daughter,

    "Tell Scabby to come here."

And he sent his daughter to bring Scabby.

When she got to Scabby she said,

    "My father says he wants you to come to him."

But the old woman was not happy with that.

She said,

    "That old man doesn't talk like people do.
    He knows my grandson can't walk around.
    My grandson won't go to him."

So when the girl went back to her father, she said,

    "Scabby can't walk.
    His grandmother told him he doesn't have to come here."

The wise man said,

    "If he can't walk himself,
    tell his grandmother to bring him here."

So the girl went back to the old woman and said,

"My father says if Scabby can't walk,
  then you should bring him."

The old woman then became more angry and said,

"Why is he sending word again that he wants to see him?
  If he wants to see him
  he can come here himself.
  I won't carry my grandson over there."

And with that she sent the girl home.

She told her father
the old woman had said she wouldn't bring her grandson.

The old man said,

"Does she think the boy will die if someone sees him?
  She's hiding him to prevent people from seeing him."

So he went over there.

[ACT I, SCENE IV]

As soon as he went in and looked at Scabby he said,

"Grandmother,
  I won't say anything.
  All of the children came to me.

"This boy here is also a child,
  so I thought I should look at him too.

"Now I'm satisfied that I've seen him.
  I'm going back home."

Nobody knew why the wise man
had asked the children go to him.
He was the only one who knew.

[ACT I, SCENE V]

A long time afterward he explained to people.

    Children who were playing had run past his door.
    He could see rabbit hair on the foot of one of them.
    He'd seen that once
    when a boy had stepped down on some wood .
    The way he stepped wasn't much
    like the way the other children stepped.

    He had made all of the children come to him
    so he could find out who it was by looking at his feet.
    But none of the other children had a foot like that.

    That's why he'd gone to Scabby.
    He saw right away that it was him as soon as he saw his feet.

    He was beyond other people,
    but the wise man could see that Scabby was hiding.
    This is what they say.

    Still the wise man didn't tell anyone.
    This is what they say.

[ACT II, SCENE I]

The wise man's son-in-law was called Thunder Maker.

    He was married to both of the wise man's beautiful daughters.
    This is what they say.

    One day Thunder Maker started to practice his powers.

    He sang for a long time and
    then he said to the people,

        "A man has been sneaking around my wife.
        I don't know who it is.

        "I have begun to practice my powers
        but I haven't learned yet who it is.

If it's somebody here,
by tomorrow I'll know that.

"Whoever it is will die."

[ACT II, SCENE II]

The next day Thunder Maker brought a hawk to life.

He made the hawk sit in front of him.
Then he said,

"All of the men must come to me."

He had the demand passed among all of the houses.
Even though all of the men went to him,
he saw nothing.

So he said,

"Make all of the boys come to me too."

So all of the boys went there too.
But again he didn't see anything.

Only Scabby had not gone to him.

Finally he said,

"Scabby has to come here too."

That made Scabby's grandmother really angry.

"They don't talk like people do.
They shouldn't think of my grandson with women.
Now it looks like they're sending for him."

But Scabby said,

"Grandmother,
I'll go to him.
I want to know why he's saying this."

He said,

"Just carry me outside,
then I'll get there on my own."

His grandmother wanted to object, but she carried him out.

So Scabby went over to the man.

[ACT II, SCENE III]

When he got close to the tepee,
the door flap was partly raised.

Scabby saw that the hawk was sitting near Thunder Maker.
When he looked at it,
the hawk ruffled its feathers.

But as soon as Scabby motioned down with his hand
for it to calm down,
the hawk smoothed its feathers back and stopped moving.

Then Scabby went inside.

After he had stood there a while,
Thunder Maker said,

"Get out of here."

So Scabby left.

[ACT II, SCENE IV]

Well, Thunder Maker started to practice his powers yet again.

He sang for a long time
but he still didn't know who had been with his wife.

All at once he said,

"It's got to be a Dogrib.
A man was lying in the blanket with her.
They enjoyed making love, but she thought it was me.
So she didn't say anything.

"Then when he was finished he got up.
He took my wife's foot
and threw it between my legs.
That's what woke me up.

"The man ran out
   but I couldn't see him very well.
   I ran after him but still couldn't see him.
   Nobody should make fun of me like this.
   It couldn't be a man who lives here,
   so it must be a Dogrib.
   Let's get up a raiding party and go after them."

Well, Thunder Maker's powers were stronger than everybody else's.

So he made himself the head of the war party
and they set out to raid the Dogribs.

[ACT III, SCENE I]

The wise man stayed home with the others
who had stayed behind.

Then he asked his wife,

"Old woman,
   do you have any sinew?
   I want to make rabbit snares."

Then when she had given him the sinew,
the wise man twisted it for rabbit snares.

It took him two full days
to string together a lot of rabbit snares on a stick.

Then he told his wife,

"Wife,
   take these rabbit snares to Scabby.
   Tell him to set rabbit snares for me."

[ACT III, SCENE II]

So when his wife had taken the snares to Scabby,
   she said to the old woman,

"Old sister-in-law,

your brother doesn't talk like people.
He said my grandson must set rabbit snares for him.

"That's why I've brought the snares here."

Scabby's grandmother was furious.
She said,

"My grandson will freeze if he gets cold because of his scabs.
Even inside he can't move."

Then Scabby told her,

"No, Grandmother.
My grandfather told me to do these snares.
I'll set the snares for him.
If I get too cold because of the scabs
I'll just come back."

So the wife of the wise man just went home.

[ACT III, SCENE III]

After she had left, Scabby said,

"I'll set the rabbit snares.
If I can't get it done,
I'll just come back.

"Grandmother,
just carry me to where the trail enters the woods."

She said,

"No!"

But he finally talked her into it,
so she took him there.

Then he said,

"Grandmother,
go back home.
I'll try to set the snares."

So she left him and went home.

[ACT III, SCENE IV]

By the middle of the day Scabby's scabs were frozen.

He was nearly dying from cracked scabs
where the blood had oozed out
and then frozen where it had run down.

That's how he returned home.

Again his grandmother was furious with the old man.

"There are so many young men living around here.
He shouldn't have made my grandson
go out in such cold weather.
Now he's nearly killed my grandson with the cold."

[ACT III, SCENE V]

That evening the wise man said,

"My grandson went out to set rabbit snares for me.
They say he nearly froze to death.
I'd better go see him."

When he got there, Scabby said,

"Grandfather,
I was nearly frozen when I was setting the snares.
I managed to get one set,
but I didn't set it very well."

"Yes, my grandson seems to have nearly frozen.
What did my grandson do with the snares?
Did you bring them back here?"

"No, Grandfather,
I couldn't hold the pole with the rabbit snares
because my hands were so cold.
I just left it there sticking up in the snow
and came home."

So the wise man said,

"Well, Grandson,
    at least now you have tried to prove yourself.
    Never mind, I guess you can't do it,"

and he left.

[ACT III, SCENE VI]

Early the next morning the wise man said,

"Wife,
    my grandson couldn't set the rabbit snares.
    I guess I'd better go set them."

He started off.

Even by the time it was dark he was not home again yet.

He didn't get home until the next day had passed
and it was long into the night.

Then he told his wife,

"Someone has set the rabbit snares for me."

He told about how he found the snares had been set.
Scabby had set them by tossing the poles high up in the tree.
That way the snared rabbits got tossed up so high
the old man had to make a hook in order to get them down.

He hooked at them
and only in that way could he get them down.

"That's why I was gone for so long."

[ACT III, SCENE VII]

Scabby had set all of the snares which he'd been given.

He'd walked around all over.
The wise man was gone two full days
because he had to go walking around everywhere,
gathering in the rabbits and fixing the snares.
This is what they say.

[ACT IV, SCENE I]

Some time after that the wise man said to his wife,

"Now I want Scabby to tend my fishnet for me."

She told Scabby.

And again Scabby's grandmother got angry,

"No! My grandson will freeze out on the lake."

But he said,

"Oh, Grandmother,
I'll go do my grandfather's net for him.
Just carry me over there in the woods.
I'll look after my grandfather's net."

Yet again she refused.
But again Scabby talked her into it.
So his grandmother carried him into the woods.

[ACT IV, SCENE II]

It wasn't long before Scabby came back again.

He seemed to be freezing.

The wise man came to him and said,

"Grandson,
did you look at my nets?

He answered,

"No, Grandfather.
While I was taking one fish out of the net,
my hands nearly froze.
The net was frozen too.
It just snapped under the water because it was frozen.

"I just left it all that way and came home."

The wise man said,

"Well, it looks like my grandson is almost frozen,"

and he went back home.

When he got home he said,

"Wife,
I understand my net froze and broke.
I'm going to go see what's happened.
Come with me."

So he and his wife set out to check the net.

[ACT IV, SCENE III]

They saw Scabby's tracks when they came onto the lake.

He had run along one side of the trail to the net.
When he saw that,
the wise man started to go along, stepping in Scabby's tracks.

Scabby had run right up to the net basin where the net was set.

There Scabby had jumped up on a piece of ice.
So when the wise man ran up to the net,
he also ran up onto the piece of ice.

As soon as he jumped onto it,
all the ice broke into pieces.
The old man fell into a hole in the water.

He was in the water a long time because he couldn't get out.

Scabby had chiseled all the ice to make it thin.
That's why the old man fell in.

Scabby had figured out what the old man would do.
That's why he had chiseled it thin.

Apparently that's what happened.
This is what they say.

Well, his wife came to him while he was still in the water there.

While she was dragging him out she scolded him,

"You're an old man.
It's ridiculous for you to try to act like a young man.
Here you're trying to test yourself like you were young.
If some other old guy jumped here into the water,
he wouldn't nearly drown himself."

He told her,

"Be quiet, wife.
It looks like the man has set my net for me again."

The old man's clothes were frozen.

He nearly froze to death.
This is what they say.

[ACT V, SCENE I]

It had been a long time since the war party had left.

Scabby said,

"Grandmother,
do you have some tanned hide?"

She answered,

"Yes."

So he said,

"If you do,
then tell the wise man's most beautiful daughter
to make moccasins for me.
Take her the leather."

She sighed,

"Oh, Grandson,
you're a pitiful sight.
A woman like that wouldn't make moccasins for you.
It would be pointless for me to take the leather to her."

But he said,

"Grandmother,
She won't have refused until she says 'no.'
Take the leather to her and see."

[ACT V, SCENE II]

So she took the leather there.

She said to the old woman,

"Sister-in-law.
I don't know what my grandson is thinking.
He said that my granddaughter sitting there
must make moccasins for him.
I've brought this leather for her."

When the girl did not speak, the wise man said,

"Yes, Daughter,
make him the most beautiful moccasins you can."

So without saying anything, the girl took the leather.

At once she started to make the moccasins.

And that's how Scabby's moccasins were made.

[ACT V, SCENE III]

After that had happened,
he said to his grandmother.

"Grandmother,
my uncles have been clubbed to death.
I'm going after them."

Now it was becoming known that Scabby could do some things.

So his grandmother didn't say anything.

He said to her,

"Grandmother,
the wise man's daughter has made me moccasins.

Put them on me.
I want to go find my uncles."

So she put the moccasins on him, and they went to sleep.

[ACT VI, SCENE I]

Early in the morning she found that his bed was empty.

He had gone.
His grandmother didn't know when he had left.

Scabby had gone after the people.

Well, those who had gone on the raid had found the Dogribs.

They charged them early in the morning.

Suddenly someone came running up from behind
and was running alongside.
He left them behind
like they were just running in the same place.

When they got to the Dogribs
they began to fight.
The fighting came right to the edge of the camp.

[ACT VI, SCENE II]

Well, three Dogrib men had Thunder Maker surrounded.

They were just about to kill him
when Scabby came running up.

He told him,

"I'm the one who snuck in with your wife.
When you were sleeping, I threw her foot between your legs
so you woke up.

"You like to say you have the strongest powers
and so you practiced your powers to find out who did it.

"At long last you decided it must be a Dogrib.

You wanted to kill them
so you made yourself a war party leader
and came after them on this raid.

"Now you're crying out like a scared little puppy,
like a puppy who can't move because it's tied up.
If I hadn't come,
you would have died.

"Your wives aren't yours anymore.
Men like you don't have women
even if there's nothing exactly wrong with them."

And he killed the Dogribs
who had surrounded Thunder Maker.

Then at once he turned around and started running back.

Well, one of Scabby's uncles who had been left behind
in the first wave of the attack thought,

"That looks like Scabby."

So he started running back again.

[ACT VII, SCENE I]

When he came to the place
where the Dogribs had started their raid,

he found all of Scabby's scabs.
Each of them was shaped like a person,
and they were lying up on tree branches.

Well, he took all the scabs down.

He got a stick and pounded them into pieces.
Then he scattered them all over the place.
Now that Scabby didn't have any scabs
he was a handsome and well-built young man.

His uncle came running to him.

His uncle had broken up all his scabs,
so he got angry with him for that.
He almost killed him.
This is what they say.

[EPILOGUE]

So Scabby became like other people,
and he was a very capable man.

Whenever he stayed with people,
they made him be in charge.
He took both of Thunder Maker's wives
and made them his own wives.
This is what they say.

Li 1928: IV.16–62 / Li & Scollon 1976: 144–179

6 Old Axe – Story One

[PROLOGUE]

There was a man called Old Axe.

> He had no special powers,
> but he was clever.
> Everything he did turned out well for him.
> Even though he lived with all different kinds of people
> he was never killed.
> This is what they say.

> He often camped with the Dogribs.
> Much of the time he stayed with his own relatives.
> This is how he lived.
> This is what they say.

Once, he was staying with the Dogribs.

> Two of the Dogribs had strong powers.
> This is what they say.

Old Axe wanted to kill them,
but he didn't know how he could do it.

> So he just went around with that group of Dogribs.

[ACT I, SCENE I]

One day he found a place where eagles were nesting.

> The eagles were nesting up on cliffs.
> Below the cliffs was a river with a big rapids.
> The eagles were nesting above the rapids.
> This is what they say.

He didn't tell anybody about this.

Then out of nowhere he asked the Dogribs,

93

"Do you have enough feathers?
If you don't, it would be good to go get some.
We'd need a lot of arrows so we could defend ourselves
if the Yellowknives suddenly attacked us."

He went around saying this among all the Dogribs.

[ACT I, SCENE II]

Now he treated those two Dogribs who had strong powers
just like his own relatives.

He pretended that he really loved them.

Whenever he went out hunting he said to them,

"Come hunting with me."

He really treated them well that way.

Because of this the Dogribs never refused him.

Old Axe said,

"If the Yellowknives came and clubbed us down,
wherever those two I love with my heart are killed,
I'll die right there with them."

He said,

"I don't want to stay on this earth
after those I love with my heart are dead."

Then he told them,

"Wherever you go
if you see eagles nesting,
tell us about it.
We'll go there to get feathers."

But the Dogribs didn't see any nesting eagles.

Then he himself said,

"Let's go a long way for feathers.

We ought to be able to find a nesting eagle.

"But don't go alone.
If you are with others and the Yellowknives charge you,
run!
The Yellowknives are not good.
You know them.

"They will attack people in raids when you least expect them.
This is known.
So look out.
Look after each other carefully."

When the time to start out came, he said,

"Those two Dogribs who have strong powers
    will come with me."

That's how they started out.

[ACT I, SCENE III]

They went a long way.

Suddenly they heard a rapids.

Old Axe said,

"If there are cliffs there,
    there must be eagles nesting.
Let's go have a look."

So they went to the rapids.

Old Axe went straight back
to where he had seen the eagle nesting.

He looked up at the edge of the cliff.

He saw an eagle's nest up there.

Well, he told the Dogribs,

"Look!
I think one of you could get to that nest."

Then Old Axe took out a lot of caribou snares.

He had brought them along with him
so they could lower people down to the nest.
He tied them all together end to end.

Then he said,

> "One of you tie on this caribou snare.
> We'll lower him down to the eagle's nest.

> "When he's gathered up the eagle feathers,
> we'll pull him back up again."

But the Dogribs told him,

> "Ol' Axe,
> we ain't gonna do nothing like that.
> It's gonna be you we're gonna lower down."

So Old Axe answered,

> "Tie the line on me, then.
> Lower me down to the nest.
> I'll get the feathers."

The Dogribs tied the snares to him,
and they lowered him down.

Old Axe gathered up many feathers,
and the Dogribs pulled him back up.

Well, then he said to the Dogribs,

> "I got a lot of feathers
> but there are still a lot down there.

> "One of you should go down.
> If those others who have gone out looking for feathers
> haven't found any,
> these we have so far won't be enough for everybody."

So one of them said,

> "Okay, Old Axe,

lower me down there.
    I'll get more feathers."

So they tied the line on one of the Dogribs
and lowered him down.

The Dogrib gathered feathers.

Then they started to hoist him up again.

Well, when they had started to lower the Dogrib,
Old Axe had set a good-sized rock nearby.

That rock was lying near him.

He told the other Dogrib to sit down in front of him.

That's how they were pulling the Dogrib up.

Old Axe grabbed the rock
        and hit the Dogrib sitting in front of him on the head.

At the same time he kicked him forward.
So the Dogrib fell off the cliff down toward the rapids.
He shouted out,

    "Hey!
    One of our relatives is falling."

The other one below shouted,

    "Hang on, Old Axe.
    Don't let me fall too!"

Well, Old Axe pulled him farther up.

When he was almost at the top,
all of a sudden Old Axe shouted,

    "There's a big bear charging me!"

And while he was shouting he beat the line against a rock
        with the other rock.

The Dogrib yelled,

"I don't care!
 Pull me up!"

But Old Axe kept pounding on the line.

Suddenly the line broke,
and the Dogrib fell into the rapids below.

That's how he killed the two Dogribs.

So he took up all the feathers himself
and started back to camp.

[ACT I, SCENE IV]

Others had already come back by the time he got home.

Then that evening he said,

"Come to me.
 I'm going to divide the feathers I brought to you."

Old Axe told all of them,

"Our two relatives who went with me
 said they were going a long way to get feathers.

"I told them,

'Don't do that. We should go together.'

"Then they told me,

'You are an old man and you'll get tired.'

"They told me to go home.

"But I told them,

'The enemy is dangerous
 so don't go far.'

"And that's how they left me.

"They are not back here yet,
but I'll put aside feathers for them.
They must not have found feathers."

Then he divided up the feathers among the people.

When he came across good feathers,

he named the two men,
kissed the feathers, and said,

"I'll set these feathers aside for them."

And so he divided up all the feathers among the people.

When he finished he put those feathers up in a birch tree.

He made two separate bundles.
Half singing and half speaking, he said,

"I have made these hoping to please these two
whom I love with my heart."

[ACT II, SCENE I]

Still the next morning those two Dogribs had not come back home.

By evening Old Axe was going around all the houses and crying,

"Something must have happened to our relatives.
They haven't come home.
Let's go look for them tomorrow morning."

Then all of the Dogribs said,

"Nah, they ain't gonna be dead.
We'll see 'em hereabouts tomorrow.
Don't you keep cryin', Ol' Axe."

But Old Axe just lay down crying.

[ACT II, SCENE II]

Before dawn the next morning he went around asking everybody,

"Have our two relatives come back yet?"

But the Dogribs called out from their homes,

"No."

So he said,

"If they aren't here,
hurry! Let's go look for them."

And with that he went all around among the people.

At every house he came to he said,

"Hurry!
Our beloved relatives still haven't come home.
They must be dead.
Hurry!"

And so he went among all the houses saying this.

When he had been to all the houses he said,

"I'm going.
My relatives who are like my own heart
aren't here.
I'm not going to just sit here and wait,"

and he left.

The Dogribs followed after him.

He went through the woods half crying, half singing.
All of the people followed him.

[ACT II, SCENE III]

Well, the people finally caught up with him.

Old Axe told them,

"They left me on that rocky hill over there.
I'll go back there with you.
From there we can separate.
Everybody should go all around and look.
If the Yellowknives have killed them, we'll find them.

"If one of us finds their bodies,
I'll go there.

I wish I could see them alive.

"But even if I don't see them while they are still living,
I want to see them in death.

"If they have died, I won't go on living.
If the people I love so much are dead,
I will die just like them."

So they separated from each other.

Even though they went all around that area
they didn't find the two men.

When they had arrived back at their camp, Old Axe cried a lot.

"I'm going to die too.
I'll go away to die alone.
I'll go away by canoe in that direction."

All of the Dogribs cried for him, grown men and women as well.
They told him,

"We love you Old Axe.
Don't go die alone."

But he started off in his canoe.

[ACT III, SCENE I]

That's how he arrived back in his own land.

When he got to his relatives he told them,

"The Dogribs are staying over that way.
They stay there because there's lots of caribou and fish.

"Let's get a raiding party after them next summer.
I've already killed the two of them who had strong powers."

So all winter he went around wherever people were staying, saying,

"Let's get a raiding party up against the Dogribs."

Finally he had gathered many people together with him.

[ACT III, SCENE II]

When spring came,
        they set out after the Dogribs with their raiding party.

Now Old Axe knew the land,
so they easily found where the Dogribs were staying.
When they came near
they saw that there were many Dogribs camping there.

Well, Old Axe told them,

    "You stay here.
     I'll go to the Dogribs in a canoe.
     When I get to them
     I'll make them all come to me on the shore.

    "When I've done that,
     you charge them from the woods.
     I'll be on the water,
     and I'll kill any of them who may go out in canoes."

So he started off toward the Dogribs.

The Dogribs were staying on a point between two lakes.
He canoed toward them along one of the lakes.
When he came into view of the Dogribs
he cried out,

    "Jack pines! Lots of them."

He was lying on his chest in his canoe.
After doing that for a long while,
he started off again.

Then suddenly he said it again.
The Dogribs who saw him said,

    "Who is it?"

One of them said,

    "There doesn't seem to be anybody there."

And they all watched.

Finally Old Axe paddled in closer to them.

They all said,

> "So this is what has become of Old Axe.
> He didn't do as he said he would."

Then while the canoe was still floating out some distance, he said,

> "A big jack pine is sticking out."

One of the Dogribs said,

> "Old Axe,
> why are you saying that?
> Come over here where we are."

But Old Axe said,

> "No!
> I was raising an orphan by myself but he died.
> The sorrow is worse than I can bear.
> I feel better if I keep calling out.
> So that's why I'm doing this."

Again he cried out, lying chest down in his canoe,

> "A big jack pine is sticking out in view."

[ACT III, SCENE III]

At last he came in close to land.

The Dogribs said,

> "Let's grab Old Axe and his canoe."

So they waded out into the water together.

Twice he paddled away from the Dogribs.

He said,

> "A big jack pine is out in the water."

He kept lying chest down in his canoe.

Well, now they were standing in the water.

> The Dogribs saw that Old Axe had something
>   covered in his canoe.
> They said,

>> "Old Axe,
>>   what is it you have covered up in your canoe?"

He answered,

>> "I'm paddling around that orphan who died.
>>   That's what it is."

He shouted out,

>> "A big jack pine is out in the water.
>>   Hurry! Hurry!"

One of the Dogribs said,

>> "Ah, this Old Axe really is pitiful.
>>   Come up to us here on land."

Old Axe yelled,

>> "Hey! A wolverine is coming right up there!"

And then they discovered that it was a shield
that he was covering in his canoe.
He took it out, held it up,
and grabbed his arrows.

He shot at them with those arrows.

At the same time Old Axe's relatives attacked the Dogribs
          from the shore.

One after another Old Axe shot the Dogribs
who tried to set out in their canoes.

Like that, not even one Dogrib got away from the shore in a canoe.

And they killed many of the Dogribs.
This is what they say.

[EPILOGUE]

Not even one of Old Axe's relatives was killed.
This is what they say.

Li 1928: v.1–36 / Li & Scollon 1976: 180–211

7 Old Axe – Story Two

[PROLOGUE]

Once, people were camped.
This is what they say.

Old Axe was staying there with them again.
This is what they say.

[SCENE I]

Old Axe spoke up and said,

> "There's a place over in the Dogribs' land
> where the caribou cross on a big lake.
> They stay there by the caribou.

> "It's a long way across that lake where the caribou cross,
> and lots of caribou swim across right there.

> "There's also a lot of fish in that lake.
> That's why they like to camp there.

> "I'm going to go over to the Dogribs' land by canoe.

> "When I get over there
> I'll get them all to gather there at the caribou crossing.

> "Then later in the summer when the berries are ripe,
> all of you come.
> Pass the news along among you.
> Get a lot of people from each place where people are camped,
> and all of you come over there.
> I'll be sure a lot of Dogribs are gathered there."

But he said,

> "If there aren't many of you,
> the Dogribs will club us all down."

So he explained to everybody
how the land was laid out in that area.

He told them,

"If you go by the direction of the big lakes
and where the big mountains are,
you'll get right to the caribou crossing."

When he had told them all of that
he himself set out for the Dogribs' land.

So his relatives passed this information among all of the others.

As a result, by summer many people had gathered together.

By the time Old Axe had told them to set out,
a lot of people set out together.

[SCENE II]

Well, at last they came to the land of the Dogribs.

They went the way Old Axe had told them to go.

There they came to a big lake.

Old Axe had said that the lake was big, so they said,

"This must be it."

They started through the woods along the shore of the lake.

Soon they came upon some sticks about two fingers long,
lying on the green moss with a little bit of dirt on top of them.

They said,

"Old Axe must have put this little bit of dirt
on top of these sticks.
Let's take a look around here."

So they all started to search.

They found another stick standing upright.

That was quite some distance up above
where they'd found the bits of dirt.
It also had a bit of dirt on top of it.

Then up above that they saw another one like it.

So they said,

> "This must be Old Axe.

> "Let's wait here for him in the woods.
> We're sure it's him who's done this.
> He wanted us to know that people are camped near here.

> "We can be sure he'll come find us here,
> so let's just wait for him."

[SCENE III]

Well, the sun was just coming up to noon.

Just then they could see someone paddling along near the shore.

It was very calm,
and he was paddling quietly along the shore toward the people.
From time to time he stopped very still,
listening to the woods.

They waited for him there in the woods.

At last he came to them.

It was Old Axe.

He stopped.
Quietly, someone whistled to him.

Old Axe made an obscene gesture at them and said,

> "Sure.
> I guess only now you've come.
> You should have got your buttocks here a long time ago.
> I had a lot of Dogribs gathered around here,
> but just about all of them took off again.

There's only one house left.
Only that one guy.
It's not going to be any fun killing just him.
He's only one person."

And he paddled up to the people.

Well, there were a lot of people sitting there in the woods.

He walked around among them.

Then he said to them,

"I see that there are a lot of you.
But there are a lot of Dogribs too.
I said there was only one Dogrib still here,
but there are really a lot of them.
We're going to have to be very careful about how we kill them."

Then he said,

"I'm going to get them to dance.

"When they're dancing tonight,
you come around on the other side of that hill
where they're camped."

He said,

"Don't let them find out about you."

Then he said,

"I'll come find you at night.
Then I'll tell you what to do."

And he went away in his canoe.

[SCENE IV]

He came to where the Dogribs were staying.

Once there, he just paddled along, crying.
It sounded close by.

When he got nearer, people said,

"Old Axe didn't used to do that.
What has happened to him?
He's come home crying."

Old Axe just cried all the more.

That's how he went back to the Dogribs.

Well, a lot of Dogribs came to him there.

One asked him,

"Why are you crying, Old Axe?"

He answered,

"Be quiet,"

and just went on crying.

Finally just about all of the Dogribs had come to him.
They spoke to him and tried to appease him.

"Old Axe,
we're happy that you're staying here with us.

"But we don't like to see you crying this way."

They all said,

"If we could do anything to make you happy
we would do that right away."

Old Axe said,

"Be quiet all of you.
When I think of all of our nice relatives the enemy has killed,
I don't really want to live on this earth any longer.

"You who are still living are not the kind of people
I like and live for.
You talk funny and you never dance.
Dancing makes people's hearts stronger
when their hearts are longing,
but you've quit dancing.

"How would somebody who is living with you
  have his heart strengthened?
  You live like you're dead.
  You must always be thinking of your own deaths.
  So even though you're still alive, my heart cries for you."

So they all said,

"Don't cry, Old Axe.
  We'll make a big feast for you tonight.
  We'll dance all night long for you."

But he said,

"You say,

    'Sure, let's dance!'

but when you've started,
  some of you will fall asleep,
  some will just sit there at home.
  It won't be long before nobody's dancing at all.
  Anybody knows that."

But they said,

"Nah, Ol' Axe.
  When we starts to dance,
  everybody gonna dance."

Old Axe answered,

"Okay,
  dance for me.

"But if you won't all dance for me,
  don't bother to dance at all."

But they all answered,

"No, we will all dance."

So Old Axe said,

"Okay."

[SCENE V]

When evening came
everybody brought their best meat and put it all together.

> When everybody had eaten well, even the children,
> they started to dance.

> Old Axe also danced among the Dogribs.

> Then he said suddenly,

>> "The Yellowknives are people,
>> but they don't behave like people.
>> We should put two men on watch."

So he took two young men
and ordered them to guarding positions away from the people.

Then he started to go around among the people.

> He made everybody dance.

> Then he said,

>> "People can't just sit there at home.
>> People are dancing here,
>> and everybody has to dance."

> So he said,

>> "I'm going to go look around the houses.
>> If there's anybody just sitting there,
>> I'll tell them to get over here to dance."

> And so he went around all the houses.

In their houses he cut most of the way through all of the bowstrings
he found there.

> He hid all of their spears.

Doing that, he went around all of their houses.

> Then he went to their canoes down at the shore.
> He used a knife to puncture all of the canoes he found there.

When he was done with that he went back to the dancing.

Then he started to dance himself and was calling out,

    "Now I'm really happy.
    This is how my relatives dance when they are happy.
    I'm glad to see this."

When he stopped he said quickly,

    "Now I'll take the place of the young man over there on watch.

    "You just enjoy yourselves here."

And he went to where the young man was guarding.

He told the young man,

    "Okay, you go back to the dance.
    You dance with the others there.
    I'll sit here and take over your watch."

But then shortly after the young man had left,
Old Axe went to look for his relatives
       where he had told them to go.

    [SCENE VI]

Well, when he found his relatives he said,

    "I've punctured their canoes
    and I have also cut their bowstrings.
    I've also hidden all of their spears.
    I've ruined all their ways of defending themselves."

Then he said,

    "When dawn comes I'll make sure they're all dancing.
    Wherever I go around among them, I'll be sure to be talking.

    "That way you'll know me."

And he went back to where the Dogribs were dancing.

[SCENE VII]

Once back with the Dogribs, he could see that it was dawning.

So he spoke out to them,

> "Now that dawn has come,
> I want you to all dance at the same time.
> Not even one of you just sit there.
> Even those two who were over there on watch
> should also dance.
>
> "I'm going to go over there
> where I can see you from a little distance."

So the Dogribs all said,

> "Okay."

And Old Axe said,

> "Good."

They said,

> "We're all dancing for him
> and that's why he's so happy now.
> We'll do just as he has said."

And all of them started to dance, even the children, everybody.

[SCENE VIII]

Old Axe stood off to one side and then said,

> "Okay, I'm happy now.
> Seeing you dance like this really makes me feel good.
> I'm not sad anymore.
> Now at last you're really dancing well."

He yelled out,

> "Now they're all dancing!"

And suddenly the ground in the woods thundered.

The Yellowknives charged the Dogribs.

Old Axe ran around among the people, yelling,

> "This is awful!
> The enemy is charging us.
> Hurry!
> Go home and get your arrows.
> Defend yourselves.
> Women and children, go escape in the canoes!"

Then he picked up his own arrows and shot Dogribs.

> The Dogribs got home.
> They got their arrows to defend themselves.

> But when they pulled their bowstrings to shoot at the enemy,
> the bowstrings all broke.

> All of their bowstrings broke like that.
> Not even one Dogrib was able to shoot an arrow.

> They didn't have any spears.
> Nothing to defend themselves with at all.

> They were all killed.

Some of them also went out in canoes, both men and women.

> When they got some distance out on the water,
> their canoes all started to sink.
> The women and children were drowning out there,
> but some men tried to swim back to land.

> Before they could get to land,
> Old Axe killed them.
> Still he was running up and down the shore,
> screaming like a crazy bear,

> > "People are drowning out there.
> > Go get the people in canoes!"

He was running up and down saying that.

The ones who started out in canoes were all drowned.

Everybody who stayed on shore was clubbed down.

That's what Old Axe did.

[EPILOGUE]

That's how he killed so many Dogribs.
This is what they say.

Since that time they first fought, many Dogribs have been killed.
This is what they say.

Li 1928: v.37–vi.8 / Li & Scollon 1976: 212–235

8 The Cannibal

[PROLOGUE]

Once, a man started out hunting.

[ACT I, SCENE I]

The sun was moving past noon.

About then he was going along on the side of a mountain.

All of a sudden he found it was hard to walk.
Even though he tried to force his way ahead,
something kept pulling him back.

He couldn't imagine what it could be.
Even though he looked all around he couldn't see anything.
He even took out his knife and passed it all around himself,
but there was nothing there.
He pushed forward, but something pulled him back.

Then he saw that someone was coming toward him across the hill.

He sat down right where he was to wait.

When that person got close enough,
the man realized it was a Cannibal.

So the man pretended that he was dead.

When the Cannibal got to him, he said,

  "That's why I planted a sharp stick to catch people."

And he grabbed the man.
He tied him up with sunbeams.
That's how he tied him up.
This is what they say.

[ACT I, SCENE II]

Well, he put the man in a coarse hunting bag
and carried him away.

He started packing him up a steep hill.

 The man was so heavy, though,
 that the Cannibal started to fart.
 That made the man laugh.

Suddenly the Cannibal said,

  "What'd you say?

  "It seems like he's still alive."

And he set the man down on the ground.

He tickled the man's palm with his fingernail.

He also tickled the roots of his teeth.

  "I guess he's not alive,
  he doesn't laugh."

So he threw him up on his back
and started off again.

[ACT I, SCENE III]

Back home, he hung up the sack with the man in it
        on the end of his cache.

Then he said,

  "Where have I seen good sticks for roasting kidneys?"

and stood there thinking.

  "Oh yeah, I saw good kidney sticks over there,"

and he started off toward the woods.

When the Cannibal had gone into the woods,
the man began to swing himself.

Doing that, the sack fell to the ground.

He climbed out of the sack,
but the Cannibal's children shouted out,

"Daddy,
your caribou is coming back to life."

While they were still yelling, the man went into the house.
He shoved hot ashes down the throats of the little Cannibals
and he put hot ashes with burning coals on the buttocks
of the Cannibal's wife.

Then he got out of there.

[ACT I, SCENE IV]

He fled terrified.

When he had crossed a good-sized lake
he looked back.
He saw that the Cannibal was already chasing him.

Then when he came to a big lake
he went way out on the lake ice.
The Cannibal also came out onto the lake.

Then it seemed that he had stopped moving.

The man thought,

"I'll go on quietly."

Before he had gone very far,
the wind came up very strong.

The Cannibal came a long way toward him.

But the Cannibal was getting hot.

He stripped off all of his clothes and threw them away.

He was chasing the man without any clothes on.

All of a sudden he yelled after the man,

"Grandchild,
wait for me!
I'm not very fast."

Then when the Cannibal was really slowing down,
he yelled out again,

"Grandchild,
wait for me!
I'm freezing cold."

But the man didn't wait for him.

Then the man went over toward the shore.

[ACT I, SCENE V]

By the time he got to the shore the Cannibal was freezing.

His jaws were shivering.
His teeth were chattering.

So he said,

"Grandchild,
light a fire.
I'm going to die.
I'm nearly frozen."

And the man thought,

"Okay, I'll light a fire.
Whatever will happen will happen."

[ACT I, SCENE VI]

Well, he lit a fire.

He piled up a lot of dry wood.
And that made it a big, hot fire.

The Cannibal came near the fire.

He said,

"Now I'm happy.
My grandchild has made a fire for me.
Without my grandchild I would not have survived."

The man kept piling on the firewood.

At last it was a huge fire.

The Cannibal was sitting by the fire warming himself
when the man came up from behind and clubbed him on the head.
He was stunned.

Quickly the man threw him into the fire.

He kept pounding him with the club.
Even though the Cannibal tried to jump out of the fire,
he kept pounding him down again.

He killed him that way, but the head kept moving.

Finally the neck was roasted
and the head fell off on one side.

But then it started to roll toward the man.
It rolled around all over the man.

Finally he threw it into the fire and got out of there.

[ACT II]

The next night when he was camping,
        suddenly something was rolling around on him.

He got up quick
because he was thinking it might be a live animal.

But it was the skull of the Cannibal.

He made another fire
and he threw the skull into it.
Again he got out of there.

The night after that the Cannibal's skull came rolling at him again
where he was camping.

Yet again he got away as quickly as he could.

Each night he kept moving away from it,
and each night the skull came rolling over him.

[ACT III, SCENE I]

Spring finally came.

By then he was completely disgusted with this thing.

Once again, he made a big fire.

He thought,

"I'm going to burn this thing up once and for all."

So he tossed it into the fire,
but the skull rolled back out of the fire.

The man grabbed it again
and threw it back into the fire.
He grabbed a heavy stick.
He pounded the skull with that.
It tried to roll out of the fire,
but the man used the club
to knock it back into the fire.

In one final whack he smashed the skull in the fire.

Something like smoke started to come out of the fire,
he couldn't tell what it was.

It made a buzzing sound which was all around him.
It covered his face completely.
It bit the man.

Even though he tried to defend himself,
they nearly killed him.

When he finally went into the smoke of the fire,
they left him.

He couldn't breathe because of the smoke.

So he came out of the smoke.

Right away they landed on him again
and started biting him again.

He didn't know what to do.

He just started running.

Whatever they were, he left them behind him.

But when he looked back, they were flying after him.
They looked like smoke.
As soon as he stopped, they caught him
and settled down all over him.

Again, he started to run away again.
But it was hot and he couldn't run very far.

At last he came to a lake.
He plunged into the water to get away from them.
Only his face was out of the water.
That's how he lay underwater.

Whatever it was following him
was like a cloud of smoke over the water.

Before long there were so many
you couldn't see through them.
This is what they say.

[ACT III, SCENE II]

Well, the man became hungry.

He couldn't stay in the water like that.

So he got up and went up onto the shore.

Everywhere he went, they were like a smoke after him.

It was impossible to go on that way.

The man made a big fire.

He discovered that whatever it was
following him around didn't like smoke.

So whenever there were too many of them,
he made a fire.

Because they avoided the fire,
it was a little better for the man.
This is what they say.

[EPILOGUE]

When the leaves change color in the fall
they disappear instantly.
This is what they say.

These are mosquitoes.
This is what they say.

The Cannibal was stupid,
and the mosquitoes were his brain.
This is what they say.

The mosquitoes were part of the Cannibal.
That's why mosquitoes like to eat people's blood.
This is what they say.

Li 1928: VI.9–27 / Li & Scollon 1976: 236–253

9   The Man Who Hibernated with a Bear

[PROLOGUE]

Once, people were camped.

When spring came, they began to make canoes.
This is what they say.

[SCENE I]

One man was nearly finished making a canoe.

He went looking for wood for the gunwales.
When he had hewed them out in the woods
he came back carrying them on his shoulder.

He was carrying them along in the woods that way.
From time to time they got caught on the branches of trees.
It was as if something was tugging him backwards.

This kept happening to him again and again.
He would go ahead,
but something would pull him back again.

He went along, thinking,

"I am getting annoyed.
I suppose it's a bear doing this."

And he looked behind him.

He found there was a bear standing there.

The bear said,

"Yes, I certainly am."

Then it said,

"Now listen!"

So the man listened.
He could hear a rapids not far away.

Then the bear asked him,

"Do you hear the rapids?"

The man answered,

"Yes."

The bear said,

"Let's go there.
There are lots of fish in the rapids.
We'll eat fish there."

Well, the man was afraid of the bear.

He thought,

"He'll kill me
if I go with him."

But quickly the bear told him,

"I won't kill you.
We'll eat fish together over there."

So he went along with him.

Finally, even though he went with the bear a long way,

the rapids still sounded about the same distance away.
This is what they say.

[SCENE II]

Then at last when the berries had ripened,

the bear said,

"Let's stay here where there are berries.
The rapids aren't far away.
We have arrived.

"When we're done here at the berries
we'll live off of the fish in the rapids."

So they stayed there at the berries.

[SCENE III]

Finally autumn came.

The bear said,

"Now let's go to the fish."

So they went.

Now it was well into autumn
when they came to the rapids in a small river.

The bear said,

"Yes, let's eat fish here,"

and it began to creep along the shore.
The man followed him.
The river was full of suckerfish below the rapids.
This is what they say.

The bear ate suckerfish, lying down at the shore.

The man also ate raw suckerfish.

He ate berries too sometimes.

[SCENE IV]

Living that way, finally winter came.

There was a little snow on the ground now.

Then the bear said,

"It looks like winter's come.
We'd better make a house."

So they left that place again.

They went a long way.

Suddenly they came across an old bear den.

The bear examined it carefully.

Then it said,

> "This is a good place.
> This will be our house.
> Now let's fix it up well."

When they had the den all fixed up,

it said,

> "Okay, we'll lie down here.
>
> "You go in first,
> and I'll come in after you."

So the man went in,
and the bear followed him in.

Then on the inside of the den
it stuffed up the entrance hole.

They lay down that way.
Once the bear had lain down, it did not move.

[SCENE V]

It lay there a long time and then it turned over.

Then from somewhere the man put a suckerfish tail in his palm.

Then it went to sleep again.

When it had slept for a long time again

it turned over again.

Once again, the man put a suckerfish tail in his palm.
This is what they say.

[SCENE VI]

A long time passed in this way.

> Then suddenly it motioned away from himself with its paw.
> Then it went to sleep again.
> A good while after that
> it turned over again.
> The man put a suckerfish tail in its palm again.

> Then it suddenly motioned toward itself with its paw.

> Soon after that they heard someone walking on the snow.

When the man came he poked a stick into the den.

The bear snorted loudly.

The man pulled the stick out and left there.

The bear said,

>> "A man has found us here in the den.

>> "Make a handprint on the snow tomorrow.
>> Make it clearly visible.

>> "Then if somebody comes here to us and says,

>>> 'How come his meat is here again?
>>> I thought it might be a person.'

>> "Then you answer back,

>>> 'There is his meat again,'

>> and go out.

>> "That way people won't do anything to you.

>> "Then they'll kill me."

Since the time when he began hibernating with the bear,
this was the first time the bear had spoken to him.

Then the bear said,

> "I have turned over here from time to time.
> I did that when the moon was full.
> All of us bears do that.
>
> "Now when I am killed,
> eat me all up.
>
> "Everybody who is camped together must eat my flesh.
> Not even a small piece of my head should be put on the ground
> under people's feet.
> My penis must also not be cut with a knife.
>
> "Anyone who would do that
> won't kill a bear again.
>
> "We bears are like one another.
> People should never laugh at us.
>
> "We don't like any of those things.
>
> "Tell that to everyone.
> That's how people will learn what we don't like."

[SCENE VII]

When morning came,
the man who had hibernated with the bear
made his handprint on the snow at the entrance to the den.

> Suddenly they heard people coming.
> When they got to the den
> one person said,

> > "How come his meat is here again?
> > I thought it might be a person.
> > Here is his handprint."

Right away the man who hibernated with the bear said,

> "His meat certainly is here."

And he went out.

Well, those people were frightened

The man told them,

> "I am a man.
> There's a bear lying right here.
> Kill it."

But everybody became suspicious.
They said,

> "This isn't like a bear.
> A person hibernated with it."

The man told them,

> "It certainly is a bear.
> Kill it.
> After that I'll tell you all about it."

So they killed the bear.
They butchered it
and packed off all of the bear meat.

Now they were suspicious of the bear meat,

but the one who had hibernated said,

> "Cook all of the bear meat.
> Then when we are sitting by the fire there
> eating the bear,
> I'll tell you how I hibernated with the bear
> and also what he has told me."

So they cooked all the bear meat.

Everyone ate together.
The man who had hibernated told everything to all the people.

[EPILOGUE]

Thus it was learned what bears do not like.

So now if a bear is killed,
they take good care of its head
and also they do not cut its penis.

That's how a man hibernated with a bear.
This is what they say.

Li 1928: VI.28–44 / Li & Scollon 1976: 254–269

10 The Adventures of Beaulieu

At first there were only two Métis staying around here.

This is what they say.

> Their French fathers came to this land by canoe.
> Two Métis came out of their marriages to Indian women.
> One of them was called Beaulieu,
> and the other was called Mandeville.

> The one called Beaulieu had strong powers.
> All of the people were afraid of him.

He was married to seven women.
This is what they say.

Even so, if he saw a beautiful woman
he would take her from her husband.

> Before he had been married to her for long
> he would send her back home.

> When he had done this throughout this land
> he set out for the land of the Slaveys.

> He said,

> > "I'll kill anybody who has strong powers.
> > And if I see a beautiful woman
> > I'll take her."

When he came to the Slaveys
he took whatever beautiful woman he saw.

> If the woman's husband said anything about it,
> he killed him.

> Then when he had not been married to that woman for long,
> he went away from those people.

133

Living in that way, he ended up
back where the Slaveys were camping.

[ACT I, SCENE I]

There he saw that there was one man who had strong powers.

He thought,

"I'll kill him.
But then I am only one person going around among strangers.
It would be better
if I had someone to go around with me.

"I'll ask this man who seems to be nearly like me in powers
if he'll go around with me,
if he'll be my partner.

"Then when I've asked him that,
if he refuses,
I'll just kill him."

So he went to the man and said,

"I go around among all the people
but right now I'm going around alone.
I haven't yet found a good partner.
I'd like you to be my partner.

"What do you think?"

For a long while the man did not speak to him.

Finally he said,

"Tell me why you are going around and
why you want me to be a partner."

Beaulieu answered,

"I'm asking you to be my partner
so I can also tell you what I'm going around after.

"Then when I've told you what I'm going after,

and if you don't like it and don't go with me,
it won't matter to me."

The Slavey said,

"Okay, tell me what you are doing."

Beaulieu answered,

"I go around among all the people,
taking any woman I like from her husband.

"If one of them says anything to me about his old woman,
I fight him.

"Then after I've given him a beating,
if he says anything further about it,
I kill him.

"And also if I hear about a person who has strong powers
I kill him too.
I use either my own hands, my powers,
or whatever I can to kill him.

"Now that's how I go around among people.

"If you want to be my partner,
you'll be my partner.

"If you think you don't want to do that,
we won't go on talking about it for long."

The Slavey did not say anything for a long time.

He just sat there.

Suddenly he spoke up,

"I'll be your partner.

"You'll be the boss.
Whatever you might say,
I'll do it.
Even if you order me to my death,
I'll do it.

"But there is one thing I have to tell you.
Don't force me to go with a woman even if she is good.
I'll only take a woman
whom I love in my own mind.

"You may think you want any woman
and you're the master of that.

"So if this is okay with you,
I'll be your partner.
If there's anything you don't like in what I've said,
then we won't be partners.

"Now tell me whatever you think about what I have said."

Beaulieu answered,

"You are just the person I want to be my partner.
You have no trouble saying what you think.
To me a man who is like that
is really a man."

And he took his hand for a moment.

Beaulieu then said,

"From today on I'm the boss.

"Now let's go visit the Dogribs."

And so he left his women behind, and they started out.

[ACT I, SCENE II]

They came to the land where the Dogribs lived.

There they made camp.

Beaulieu said,

"I have some small powers
and I can use them a little to defend myself.
If I decide to take a man's woman,
it isn't difficult for me to do that.

If we fight with our hands,
only a strong man can overpower me.

"If other people join in to help,
even if it is two or three men,
it isn't hard for me to kill them.

"Because that's the way I am,
I'm looking around here
for a woman people think is extremely good
and who also has strong powers.
I think I'll take her.

"Of course a woman like that will be married to a man
who is extremely capable in everything.
So if I see someone married to a woman like that
I'll kill him at once and take the woman.

"When people are camped together,
the boss is the man they think is above the others.

"If the time has come to take the woman from that man,
he is going to say that he'll kill us.
He may order his men to do it.

"If they do that,
will you be able to defend yourself?"

The Slavey answered him,

"I can't defend myself with my powers.
But if there are many people, even three one after the other,
if I focus my mind on them while I speak,
they won't have much strength.
Also I can focus my mind on them,
and they will do what I want them to do.
If the time comes that a man decides to fight,
I can also defend myself a little.
This is how I am.
It's not like you were alone.
I can defend you a little, though not much."

[ACT II, SCENE I]

So they went to look for the Dogribs.

In time they came to a camp with many Dogribs.

Beaulieu said,

"We won't do anything to these people.

"That's how we'll come into their camp.
If they don't do anything to us,
we'll stay with them.

"If I find a woman I like
I'll just take her.

"If I don't see one like that,
we'll stay here with them a long time.
And after that we will leave them."

Then he said,

"Always be ready
from the time we arrive there with these people.
Be ready in case they do something quickly.
We'll be thinking about how we can kill them."

So they went to the camp.

When they came into the Dogrib camp,
the Dogrib people were afraid of them.

Even though they came as strangers
they acted bravely.
Having no fear,
even though there were so many of them,
they came among the Dogribs.

Beaulieu said,

"We were out hunting by ourselves.

"We have ended up far from our home,
but we haven't found anything to kill,

so now we are very hungry.
There are a lot of people here,
so it seems you must have a good supply of meat."

At once a Dogrib said,

"Two hungry strangers have come to us.
Bring whatever good meat we have.
Let the strangers eat well."

Right away good meat and many caribou tongues
were brought from the homes that were around there.

When the meat was cooked,
all the aged ones who were staying there
gathered together.

They ate very well.

One of the old men said to Beaulieu,

"Grandson,
your land is far away,
but you have come here to us.
What were you hunting for?"

Beaulieu answered,

"We had no meat at home
so we went out hunting.

"When we had gone a long way,
a heavy snowstorm came up.

"We continued on,
but we didn't know where we were going.

"Finally it seemed that we had come a long way
away from our land,
but we kept on going
because we thought we might kill something ahead.

"That's how we ended up here.
Grandfather,

if we hadn't come here to you
we would have died without any meat to eat.

"Apparently there are caribou around here.
You seem to be living well here on good meat.
Back there where we came from
we haven't seen any caribou tracks at all."

Well, the old man started to become suspicious of them.
He said,

"It is a wonder that they have lost their way."

Beaulieu responded,

"If we had lost our way
we wouldn't have come here to you.

"Now we have come here.

"It's not like we had become lost.
It's no great wonder when somebody comes
to the camp of others.
I came here because I thought it would be nothing to you
if someone came because you were ordinary people.

"Now it seems that it is a wonder to you
that we have come.
If you are alive in the future,
you may see even greater wonders than this."

The Dogribs didn't say anything, so Beaulieu also remained silent.

So they slept there with the Dogribs.

When morning came, Beaulieu said to the Dogribs,

"We won't sit here with you all the time.
We'll go walk around the homes off a way from here
where people are staying.
After we visit all of the people,
we'll go back to our land."

So they started to go around visiting.

In the middle of the camp there was one tepee
which was the biggest one of all.

When his partner saw it standing there, he said,

"Cousin Beaulieu,
there's a tepee over there.
Let's go.
It looks like the home of a man who is very well off."

So they went in there.

The man seemed remarkably well-to-do.
Two women were married to him.

There was also an unmarried young man staying there inside.

Besides him there was another man who was married
but still looked like a young man,
sitting with his wife across the fire from the well-off man.

That's what Beaulieu and his partner met when they went inside.

When they had come in, the Dogrib said,

"Sit down."

As soon as they had sat down, Beaulieu said to the Dogrib,

"I didn't come to sit for a long time.
I'll be leaving for my own land soon.

"But I don't like to have come here to this land for nothing.

"It looks to me like you have two women.
Give me one and I'll be very pleased."

Well, the Dogrib answered angrily,

"Oh! Oh! I also think I'm a man.
That's why I have married two women.
I don't care at all about other people!"

So Beaulieu answered him,

"If you give me the woman,
I'll love her just as you have loved her."

The Dogrib answered back,

"We don't just give women to others like that.
I'm not going to give you a woman!"

Beaulieu just got up and took one of the women.
He picked her up,
and he put her down by where he was sitting.

Then he told the Dogrib,

"Were you worried I might take her?
I've already done that.
That's all there is to it."

The Dogrib answered,

"I guess you think you're a man.
Well, I am too.
I don't think you will take a woman from me like that."

And he got up.

Beaulieu said,

"Just sit there!
Don't say another word!
If you say anything else,
I'll take both of your wives."

At once the Dogrib started to speak,
but before he could say anything,
Beaulieu grabbed him and threw him out of the tepee.

Well, the Dogrib was enraged.
He went around complaining to everybody,

"Those two strangers who came here
have thrown me out and taken my women.
Come with me.
Let's make him see what he is looking for."

Right away many Dogribs came to Beaulieu.

"This man is the master of all of us who stay here.

"We won't let a stranger treat him this way.
   Come on out of there!"

Beaulieu said,

"Don't even one of you come inside here.
   This is my home.
   All of you go back to your own homes."

The Dogrib whose home it was said,

"Too much! Let's give him a lesson!"

And he started to go into the tepee.

Well, before he was halfway in,
Beaulieu punched him in the head.

The Dogrib collapsed.
Beaulieu grabbed him and threw him outside.

Another Dogrib poked his head inside,
and he punched that one in the head too.

He was stunned and fell outside the tepee.

The Dogribs said to each other,

"This is too much!
   Let's kill him."

Then the Slavey yelled out to the Dogribs,

"Get back to your homes, all of you.
   Anyone who hangs around here is going to die.
   It looks like you are saying that you want people to die.
   If you stay around here,
   not one of you will see his home again."

His voice was loud.
It thundered out again,
and the Dogribs were terrified of him.

So they turned and started back to their homes.

They said,

> "We thought those were people who came to visit us,
>   but they do not seem like people.
>   We'd better leave them alone,
>   or they'll kill us."

They carried those two Dogribs
that Beaulieu had hit and who were lying unconscious
away to their homes.

They all went home.

Beaulieu said to the two men who were still sitting there inside,

> "You don't need to be afraid of us.
>   We won't do anything to you.
>   You will work for us
>   and do whatever we order you to do.
>   Cook for us and
>   also keep a good stack of firewood at the door.

> "We're not going to work anymore at all."

And that's how they stayed there.

> "There's no meat?
>   Go get it from the other houses."

At once they would bring meat to them.

Well, the Dogribs finally all said,

> "Let's kill them.
>   There is no reason for us to have them stay here with us."

The man whose wives were taken from him was very sick.

> He had nearly died from being beaten by Beaulieu.
> When he got well enough to get around again,
> he said,

> "This is too much!

> "Their hands are strong,
>   but it might be possible to kill them with weapons."

They talked about Beaulieu where he couldn't hear them,
but the partners knew everything that was said.

Finally it was said that they would be killed.

When the time came, Beaulieu said to his partner,

"Partner,
get yourself ready.
Today we are going to see what we came here for.
But they won't kill us.
I have already seen that we have left here.
If they try hard to kill us
they'll be the ones who die.

"If they don't do that,
we'll only kill those who have done the most."

Well, they got up early the next morning.

The sun had already come up,
but nobody was doing anything yet.

Impatiently, Beaulieu said,

"Partner,
when something is going to happen,
it's best if it happens quickly.
I want to hurry along
what they have said will be done to us.
Let's go after them."

His partner agreed immediately,

"I'm really getting impatient too."

So they went right then to the Dogrib
from whom he had taken the women.

They went right in.
And so that all the Dogribs could hear him,
Beaulieu shouted out loudly,

"It looks like you want more people to die.

You're going around saying,

    'I'll kill people,'

but that's just talk.
If a man wants to kill someone,
he just does it.
He doesn't just go around talking about it all the time.

    "Now you're going to get what you want."

And he punched him in the head.

Rapidly he kneed him into the ground
and grabbed hold of the man's hair.
He twisted his neck,
and they heard his neck snap.
When he let go,
his head flopped over to one side.

Everyone inside the tepee jumped up.

Together with his partner they punched the Dogribs,
and they collapsed.
They were crying out,

    "The strangers are killing us all!
    Get in here in a hurry!"

But in the end they killed everybody who was there inside.

They went out of the tepee.

Already there were some Dogribs waiting there, holding arrows.

The Slavey told them,

    "Don't shoot even one of those arrows you're holding.
    Anyone who shoots an arrow will be shot himself."

Not one arrow was shot.

One of them thought,

    "I'll give it a try."

But Beaulieu took out a mink skin.
He held it by the head and swung it at the Dogrib
who was positioning himself to shoot.

As soon as he did this,
the Dogrib collapsed on the ground
with the blood gushing out of his throat.

Well, they ended up killing many of the Dogribs.

The Dogribs were terrified
so they ran inside their tepees to hide.

They went around among the Dogribs
and killed everyone they came to.
The Dogribs didn't defend themselves,
so they killed all of them.

So they went back to their tepee.

When they got there, Beaulieu told the two women,

"A lot of people have died because of you.
But it's not your fault,
so we'll let you live."

He went on,

"I won't kill these two men who have worked for us either."

He turned to his servants and said,

"You've worked hard for me,
so I'll let you live.
Now you keep these two women.
Be sure to treat them well.
My partner and I are going back to our own country,
but next winter we'll come back here again.

"You'll see us again then."

Then he said,

"Be sure to tell any Dogribs you see
about everything that has happened here."

That's what he said to them.

And in that way they started back.

[ACT II, SCENE II]

When they returned to their land,
Beaulieu took two women from his relatives.

He lived with them.

When the ice was frozen hard on the inland lakes in autumn,
he said to his partner,

"Partner,
  let's set out again for the land of the Dogribs.
  I want to see those two women again."

So they set out for the land of the Dogribs.

When they got to the land of the Dogribs,
they came to a camp with many Dogribs.

The Dogribs had already heard about them,
so when they arrived there
nothing was said.
There were many Dogribs staying together there,
but they were all afraid of him.
They knew that they were said to be very strong men.

Because of this Beaulieu took any woman he liked.
He just went inside,
took the woman's hand,
and left without saying anything at all.

When he'd taken her back to his own place
he told her,

"Don't leave here!
  I'm your husband from now on."

That's how he lived among the Dogribs.

Even if her husband was sitting right there,

if he liked a woman
he just took her hand and left.

Even so the Dogribs didn't say anything
because they were terrified of him.

That's how he came to have seven women staying with him.

They stayed with the Dogribs for a long time.

Then they heard
that there was a large camp of Dogribs in another place.

Beaulieu said,

"Partner,
    tomorrow we're going to the place
    where they say the Dogribs are.
    Those two women that I took are probably staying there."

And right then he led the first woman he'd taken
        back to her husband.

He said,

"My rival,
    here I have brought your woman back to you.
    I'm happy that she stayed with me.

"Now I'm going away again.
    If we're still alive
    maybe we'll see each other again.

"Be sure you treat your wife well."

When he'd gone around and said that to all the other men
he gave their women back.

[ACT II, SCENE III]

Before dawn the next morning they left.

They arrived at the camp where those people were staying.
They found that both of the women he had married were there,

each one married to one man.
Beaulieu and his partner went to look for them.

Right away they heard where they were staying
and just went right in.

He told that Dogrib,

> "Get out of here.
>   This is my place from now on.
>   I'm going to be married,
>   and you'll work for me."

The Dogrib was terrified,
so he didn't say anything.

He just got up
and moved to the other side of the fire to sit.

Then Beaulieu turned to the other woman
and took her again.
He told her husband,

> "Come with me to my place.
>   Work for me there."

Then he just went back out with the woman.

When he got back to his home,
the Dogrib came along, following him.

Beaulieu told both of those men,

> "Don't think about these women
>   as long as I am staying here.
>   I am their master.
>   You work for me.
>   Stay here with me."

And so he went on taking any woman he liked.

He took many women, so finally the Dogribs said,

> "This is too much!
>   As long as he is the master of our wives,

we're living here without women.
This isn't right.
Let's go get the women back."

One Dogrib saw the woman who had been his wife outside.

"You were my wife.
You should come back with me right now."

Beaulieu heard him.

He ran out and beat him nearly to death.

That really angered the Dogribs.

Because of their anger,
Beaulieu and his partner killed many Dogribs.
Still they did not kill half of those who were staying there.
Then again they started out away from those people.

They heard about where more Dogribs were staying.

So they went from place to place among all the Dogribs.
They took women
and they killed men.

Moving around that way they came to Great Bear Lake.

From there they headed back to their own land.

This is how they lived,
and because of the way they lived,
they killed many Dogribs.
This is what they say.

[ACT II, SCENE IV]

They stayed again in their own land for a long time.

There was a woman who was with the Hares.
She had very strong powers.
She was also more beautiful than any other woman.
Because of that she had married the two Hare men
who had the strongest powers.

This is what they say.

Beaulieu and his partner heard about her.

Beaulieu said,

> "Okay, partner,
> this is a woman just like we have been looking for.
> Let's go see about that.
>
> "We have never known anywhere in this land
> a woman who is married to two men.
>
> "This woman must be very strong.
> Let's go look for her tomorrow.
> We'll soon see what they mean."

So they started off the next day.

In time they came to where that strong woman was staying.

The two men really were capable men.

> They had killed moose
> and had a lot of meat.

Beaulieu said,

> "Let's not kill this woman's husbands in front of her.
> They say she has very strong powers.
> That might be true.
> They've gone off hunting,
> so we'll go hunting too.
>
> "If we see them out there
> we will kill them then."

The next day Beaulieu said,

> "My partner and I are going out to hunt.
> We have eaten up much of your meat.
> It is already becoming difficult for everyone."

They set out hunting the next day.

They set out after the Hares.

They came to the Hares after they had gone a long way.

They killed them right there.

Then Beaulieu returned.

Right away he took the woman.

From then on Beaulieu and his partner did not hunt.
They just lived on the meat which was already there.

In time they ate up all of the meat.

Beaulieu said to his partner,

> "There isn't any meat now,
> but don't kill a moose.
> For a long time they have said
> that we may have killed the men.
> So they know about us.
> But they have said nothing.
> When they say something,
> then we'll kill them."

The people hunted because there was no meat
but they found nothing.

In the end it was impossible to stay there,
so the people went out.

For three days the wind was good for hunting.

Beaulieu and his partner started hunting.

They returned in the evening,
but they didn't find anything.

When he came inside he said,

> "The wind is good, but I haven't killed anything."

Well, the woman's mother was staying with them.

The old woman said,

> "They say that this stranger can do anything.

There was good meat here before.
Now it looks like we will starve with this stranger."

Beaulieu immediately grabbed his big knife.

He said,

"Partner,
it looks like this is what we were waiting for."

He stabbed his wife.
But the body he'd just stabbed got up
and started to go out with blood streaming out of it.

So Beaulieu grabbed her again.
He fought with her,
but she was so strong he couldn't throw her down.

He grabbed his knife again
and chopped the woman's neck.
He severed her neck tendon.
The woman groaned and fell on her face.

Beaulieu cut her head off.

He threw the head off to one side.

Even though the head was now lying far away from the body,
she moved her eyelids.
The headless body began crawling over to the head.

Beaulieu said,

"It doesn't seem possible to kill her with a knife.
Make a big fire."

When the Slavey got a big fire going,
they threw the woman's body and her head into the fire.

Then Beaulieu said,

"Partner,
we have finished what we started out to do.
Let's go home."

And they started home.

154

[ACT III, SCENE I]

The evening after they returned home,

Beaulieu said,

> "Partner,
> I wanted to kill those people who thought
> they were better than others.
> And I wanted to be the master to any woman
> who was above others.

> "Well, enough. I've done that.
> But it isn't any use to us.
> I won't give up women,
> but now I've killed enough people.
> I'm done with that.

> "If you want to stay together as partners,
> that's fine.
> But if you think you'd rather stay alone,
> that's up to you."

The Slavey answered,

> "I have killed a lot of people because of you
> but I'm happy to have stayed with you.
> Now I'll stay here in my own land.

> "It's best for you to go back to your own land.
> I can defend myself from people like me,
> even without you.

> "You are also like that.
> There's no reason we can't stay alone without each other."

So they took each other's hands for a moment,
and Beaulieu left him there.

[EPILOGUE]

Well, when Beaulieu got back to his own land
he took a woman.

    Not long after that he took another one.

    He ended up taking many women.
    He kept the ones he liked
    and rejected the women that did not appeal to him.

    In that way he came to have many women.

Then the first priest came into this land.

Beaulieu was married to seven women at the time he came.

    They all lived with him.

The priest told him of God's teachings.

    So Beaulieu was converted.
    He left six of the women,
    and then the priest married him to just one of them.

From that time on he fervently prayed for himself.

    He also made penance.
    He had learned that God did not approve of his killing people.

    He said,

      "I'll make penance for my sins.
      Wherever I have killed people
      I'll go there making penance."

    When he had done that,
    then he just stayed in one place.

He lived for a long time and died well,
having seen his children grown.

Li 1928: VI.45–VIII.16 / Li & Scollon 1976: 270–321

11 The Man Who Became a Wolf

[PROLOGUE]

There was a man called Spread Wings.

> From time to time he became a wolf.
> This is what they say.

> After he has been a wolf,
> when he becomes a man again,
> he becomes a young man.
> This is what they say.

> Three times he has lived to be an old man.
> This is what they say.

This is the story he told about becoming a wolf again.

[SCENE I]

When he was very old, a wolf spoke to him,

> "If you want to live longer on the earth
> you must live with us again.
> If you do that you will live for a long time."

Spread Wings thought,

> "I don't want to be a wolf again."

But the wolf said,

> "If you do not become a wolf again
> you will die soon."

Spread Wings answered,

> "I want to live longer on the earth,
> so I will become a wolf again."

He immediately became a wolf.

Then he realized that the wolf
who was speaking to him
was an old woman.

As soon as Spread Wings had become a wolf,
the old woman said to him,

"Grandson,
    there are probably many caribou up north.
    Let's go that way."

[SCENE II]

They started north.

Although the wolf was old, she went fast.
So they came to the end of the big lake in no time.
And doing so they finally came again to the barren ground.

Suddenly they saw caribou tracks.

His grandmother said,

"Grandson,
    we are hungry now.
    These tracks we are seeing were left by meat.

"I am old, and so it is impossible for me,
    but you are a young man.
    It is not impossible for you.
    You go after it.

"I'll start after you.
    If you kill a caribou,
    I will come to you."

Spread Wings started after the caribou.

They came to the barren ground,
    but there were still small pockets of woods.
    He tracked the caribou among them.

He tracked a long way in the moonlight on the barren ground,
and then there was a small woods in one place.
The caribou tracks went in there.
He thought,

"The caribou must be lying in there."

He set off to the downwind side.
He came around downwind of the woods,
and there were no caribou tracks.

He thought,

"They must be in there."

Quietly he crawled forward into the woods.

He had crawled nearly through the woods,
far enough that he could see through to the other side.
He saw a caribou lying close to the trees.

Quietly he crawled toward it.

As he came out of the woods,
he was very close to it.
But he thought,

"If it saw me
and it jumped up away from me,
I couldn't kill it."

So he looked carefully at the ground between him and the caribou.

He crawled to a place where

if the caribou jumped up and came down,
and then jumped up again,
he would be there to spring upon it.

He sprang toward the caribou from there.

The caribou saw him.

It jumped up suddenly,
but the wolf also jumped again.

He lunged at the caribou
and caught its throat in his teeth.
The caribou tried to jump again
with the wolf's teeth clamped on his throat,
but the wolf was chewing on his throat.

Finally the caribou became sluggish
and slumped to the ground.

Then Spread Wings released his grip on the throat of the caribou.
He looked back.
His grandmother had the caribou's leg tendon in her teeth.
She said,

> "Grandson,
>   tear open its stomach.
>   It'll get up again."

Immediately Spread Wings bit into the caribou's stomach.
He tore at it.

His grandmother bit in alongside of him.
They yanked away from each other.
And so they tore the caribou open.

The caribou died.

The old woman said,

> "Grandson,
>   now we've made meat.
>   We'll sing,
>   then we'll eat.
>   If anyone who is hungry is nearby
>   he will hear us.
>
> "If someone hears us
>   he'll eat with us."

And so she started to howl.

She howled for a long time,
but there was no one.

"Grandson,
  there doesn't seem to be anyone.
  If somebody was near here
  he would have come already,
  but no one is here.

"Now we'll eat."

And they began to eat.
They ate half of the caribou.

The old woman said,

"Grandson,
  we have not eaten for a long time.
  If we eat more now
  we will overeat.

"We'll sleep now.
  Then we'll eat more."

They lay down to sleep.

After they had slept a long time,
the old woman said,

"Grandson,
  now let's eat again."

So they ate more.
They ate up nearly all of the caribou.

Finally when there were only bones lying around,
the old woman said,

"Grandson,
  if there aren't many caribou,
  people will get hungry.
  We'll cache these bones here where the game was killed.
  If anyone who is hungry comes along
  he'll have this to eat."

So they put all of the bones in one place
and piled snow up on them,
and the old woman said,

"Grandson,
   now we'll leave here.
   This probably isn't the only caribou.
   There may be many caribou ahead."

So they started out again.

They went a long way,
but there were no caribou tracks.

At length they became hungry.
The old woman said,

"Grandson,
   there don't seem to be any caribou tracks.
   We'll go over to the woods again.
   If we can kill a moose
   we'll eat well.
   There are no caribou around here."

[SCENE III]

They started for the woods again.

They went a long way,
but there were no caribou tracks in the barren ground.

"In the woods there are probably many caribou.
There are none around here."

At last they came into the woods,
but there were no caribou.

After so long they had become hungry,
but they did not see any tracks.

Far into the woods,
they saw some moose tracks at last.

The old woman said,

"Grandson,
   this is meat.

We're very hungry,
so we'll follow it and track it."

They started out after it.

When they had tracked it a long way
they came upon fresh moose tracks.

She said,

"Grandson,
I'm so hungry that I'm not very strong.

"You track it.
I'll follow you."

Spread Wings began to track the moose.

After he had tracked it a long way
he started around to go downwind of it.

Suddenly the moose caught his scent,
so he moved directly toward it.
He got close,
but he was weak
because he was so hungry.
He thought,

"It's going to be impossible for me to kill the moose."

He continued to follow the moose.
When he came close behind in the woods
he leaped toward the moose.
But the moose leaped forward,
and he missed catching it by the throat.

The moose had moved too quickly for him to catch his throat,
so he couldn't do it.

At the last moment he caught the moose's leg tendon.
The moose ran while he held on with his teeth.
Before the moose could take more than a few steps,
his grandmother had caught the moose's throat.

The moose kept running with them hanging on.

Finally the moose stopped.

The old woman said,

"Grandson,
   tear its insides open.
   I'm so weak
   I can't hold it in my teeth for long."

Spread Wings bit into the moose's stomach.
He chewed and pulled it.

He tore through the stomach.
The intestines spilled out.
The moose collapsed.
The old woman had already torn out its throat,
so the moose died.

The old woman said,

"Grandson,
   we won't eat.
   We'll just drink a little blood.

"We'll lie down
   and after that we'll eat.
   We've come so far that I'm exhausted and weak.

"We haven't eaten in a long time,
   so there is no meat in our stomachs.
   If we eat too much
   we'll get sick from overeating."

After they had drunk some blood
and eaten a little meat
they lay down.

When she had slept the old woman got up and said,

"Grandson,
   let's eat now.
   It's a fat moose,

but don't eat too much fat.
Let's just eat a little meat."

And so they ate and lay down again.

Before they had slept long,
the old woman got up and said,

"Grandson,
get up. We're going to eat again."

They went to where the dead moose was lying.

The old woman said,

"Grandson,
we killed the moose
but we ate
before we had sung.

"Now we'll sing
and then we'll eat."

The old woman started to sing.

She sang for a long time and then said,

"Grandson,
now we'll eat our fill."

And they both ate their fill.

Then the old woman said,

"Grandson,
we have become skinny
because we haven't eaten meat for a long time.
Let's stay here until we eat up all of this moose.

"When we get strong again
we'll start out again."

So they stayed there
until they had eaten up the whole moose,
and then started out again.

[SCENE IV]

Winter finally passed.
　　As the days became longer
　　the old woman said,

　　　　"Grandson,
　　　　　it is a long way to the barren ground.

　　　　"Now that it is spring,
　　　　　they are gathering there
　　　　　in order to mate.
　　　　　Let's go there."

So they started out again.

　　After some time it was getting warm,
　　and water was floating on the ice.

　　The old woman said,

　　　　"Grandson,
　　　　　the time for mating
　　　　　has come there.
　　　　　I am in a hurry to get to where they have gathered in the north."

　　And she started off.
　　She took off really fast from there.

　　She left the man behind,
　　and the way she was going,
　　they soon came to the distant barren ground again.
　　　She stopped on a mountaintop.

She said,

　　　　"Grandson,
　　　　　listen!"

Spread Wings listened.
He heard wolves howling from a distance.

　　　　"Grandson,
　　　　　they are talking.

"Let's go quickly over there where we hear them."

And she started right out.

At last they came to a sand hill where there were a lot of wolves.

The boys and girls who were not mating were staying there.
The ones who were mating were on the opposite side
    of the sand hill.
As soon as he caught up with the old woman, she said,

"Grandson,
    you stay here with them.
    I'm going over where the others are."

At once she started over to the other side.

So he stayed a long time with the boys who were there.
Then his grandmother came back to him.

She said,

"Grandson,
    they are all finished now.
    They are all going their separate ways.

"We'll go up onto the sand hill.
    After we have all sung together
    we'll go off on our separate ways."

And so everyone gathered together with her.
Up on top of the sand hill
after they had sung together for a long time,
his grandmother said,

"Grandson,
    we'll head south again now.
    These people are going up north."

And so they started again.

They went a long way again.

The old woman said,

"Grandson,
we'll make a den here."

When the den was ready,
she told him,

"Grandson,
I will stay here.
You go away and hunt for yourself.

"When the summer berries have grown,
come back.
It should not be far from here.
If you have killed something,
bring the meat to me here.
But don't come inside."

So Spread Wings set out away from his grandmother.

When he had been away from there for a long time
he returned.

His grandmother was standing outside,
and she saw him coming.

She said,

"Grandson,
apparently you are still alive.
I'm hungry.
I hope you've killed something."

He answered,

"I have killed a caribou not far away.
It's all lying there."

The old woman said,

"Grandson,
let's go there.
I'll eat from it."

So they went.

When they got to the caribou
they ate.
Then she pulled a caribou hindquarter along,
and they returned to the den.

The old woman said,

    "Grandson,
      look inside here."

So Spread Wings looked inside.
He saw the old woman's four pups were inside there.
She said,

    "Grandson,
      these are your nephews.
      Until they are able to hunt themselves,
      the two of us will hunt for them."

So that's how they stayed there.

     [SCENE V]

By the time autumn had come, the pups had grown large.
The old woman said,

    "Grandson,
      your nephews can't hunt
      but they can walk around.
      So if we leave here
      it will be okay.
      We have killed everything around here.
      It isn't possible for us to stay here now."

They all started out.

When they came into the woods
they came among many caribou.

They followed the caribou around wherever they went.
During that winter the pups learned to kill caribou.

So the old woman said,

"Grandson,
it isn't impossible for these nephews of yours to kill caribou.

"Now let's go south.
So they can learn to kill moose too.

"After that they can live alone."

So they headed south.

They went far into the woods.
When they saw moose tracks,
the old woman said,

"Grandson,
you track the moose,
and your nephews will go along with you.
You teach them how to kill a moose.

"If it isn't too far to the moose,
you have them kill it themselves."

She told her pups,

"Moose aren't like caribou.
They have tough skins and they are strong.
But if one of you bites into its leg tendon
and one of you bites into its throat,
it can be killed quickly.

"You must watch its feet carefully
to keep from being kicked.

"That's how you kill a moose.

"Now you go after a moose.
I'll come along behind you."

They started out after a moose.

At length they came to fresh moose tracks.

Spread Wings told them,

"Come quietly behind me.

I'll go after it.
When I get to it
I'll wait for you."

So he started after the moose.

Before long he came to a moose which was lying down.
He lay looking at it where it was lying in the snow.

Before long the young wolves crawled up behind him.

He whispered quickly,

"You kill it.
I'll be right behind.
Go quickly.
If he got up
he'd be impossible to catch
because he'd really move fast."

All four of the pups jumped it at once.

Before the moose had got up,
one pup got its throat.
Two pups bit into a leg tendon.
The remaining one paced back and forth in front of it.
It was impossible for the moose to go forward.

Finally it bit into the moose's nose.
Before long the moose collapsed where it was,
and they killed it.

When the old woman caught up with them
she said,

"Children,
you have killed a moose.
I am happy.
Now we'll all sing
and then we'll eat."

At once she started singing.
They all sang.

And then they ate.
They ate up all the moose.

Then they started out again.

Even though they went a long way
they did not kill anything.

Finally they came to a place where people were staying.

They went around to all the places
where game had been killed
and ate the snow in those places.
Other than that no food touched their mouths.

In the end they were not able to kill anything.

They had become very weak.

The old woman said,

"Grandson,
you have stayed with us again for a long time.

"Go back to live with your relatives again.
If you hunt and kill something,
always leave a little meat for us.
Remember this as long as you live when you kill something.

"Now we'll sing,
and then you go back to your people."

They all sang for him,
and then Spread Wings left them.

[EPILOGUE]

He saw a man walking along on a lake.

He approached the man on four legs.
When he got close to him,
the man reached for his gun, thinking,

"I'd better shoot it."

The wolf said,

> "Don't kill me!
> I am one of your people."

The man was scared
so he didn't shoot.

Spread Wings said,

> "Go back to your home
> and I'll follow you.
> I'll wait for you nearby.
> Bring me some men's clothing from your home."

The man said nothing when he got home.

He went back to the wolf,
taking men's clothing with him.

When he had returned,
the wolf told him,

> "I look like a wolf
> but I am a man.
> Don't be afraid of me.
> Wait over there in the woods for me.
> When I have finished dressing
> I'll come back to you.
> We'll go back to the people together."

So the man did as he was told,
and after the wolf was dressed,
he came back to the man.
Together they went back to the people.

Spread Wings told the people about how he had been a wolf.

That's how he became a person again.
This is what they say.

Li 1928: VIII.16–IX.10 / Li & Scollon 1976: 322–357

12 The Cheating Gambler

[PROLOGUE]

There was a man named Pierre Dry-Tendon.

He won a lot from many people playing the hand game.
This is what they say.

Many people played against him, one after another,
but there was never anyone who could win.
He won tobacco, clothing, ammunition,
        and many other such things.
This is what they say.

Finally behind his back people started to say,

"He must be cheating.
    That's how he wins so much at the hand game."

[SCENE 1] ·

The next time they were playing the hand game
they watched him carefully.

They guessed which hand the object would be in
but they guessed wrong.

One after another they played and made their guesses,
but none of them was able to guess correctly.

When the next person came to play against him,

before he had made his guess,
one of them grabbed both of his hands.

He thought,

"I'll pull my hands out."

But the man who had grabbed him was strong,
and he was unable to pull his hands away.

The man who had grabbed him looked into his palm.

He held a button in each hand.

They were tied together with a thread.
The thread was strung through his sleeve,
passed over his neck,
and run down the other sleeve.

That way he had held a button in each hand.
If one side was guessed,
by pulling the thread to one side with one of his hands,
it went into his sleeve.
That way he made it seem to people
that there was nothing in his palm.

That was how they discovered
he was winning so much from people.
Everybody became very angry with him.

[SCENE II]

Then he became ashamed of himself
and began to cry like a child in front of everyone.

The people who had played with him on his side
had also won a lot.
But some of them were good people and they said,

"We thought he was playing fairly,
but he wasn't.
We will give back all of the things we have won."

They gathered together all of the things they had won.

They said,

"You people know which things are your own.
Take your own things back."

So they recovered their things.

The cheating gambler then said,

"I'll also give people's things back."

But people got very angry with him.
They told him,

"Right now you are lying again.
Now that we know how you've stolen things
we won't take them back.
Go to hell with all of these things you have stolen!"

[EPILOGUE]

So after staying at the fort for the summer, they set out again.

Before they had gone far, Dry-Tendon became sick.
He was in pain all summer,
and when autumn came
he died.

Even in gambling there is no luck for someone who cheats.
This is what they say.

If people gamble, they should do it fairly.
This is what they say.

Li 1928: IX.11–18 / Li & Scollon 1976: 358–363

13 The Flight of the Last Dogribs

[PROLOGUE]

A man was walking alone.

[SCENE I]

The man came to a great lake.

> He saw that there were tracks of some people,
> and it seemed to him that they were Dogrib people.
> So he ducked back into the woods.

> There he climbed up to the top of a hill
> and he could see Dogribs
> sitting at fishing holes on the lake.
> The holes extended in a line out onto the lake.

He thought,

> "They'll kill me if they discover my tracks."

By the time evening came he had piled up spruce boughs

> here and there throughout the woods
> on the side of the hill.

> In the evening when he saw the Dogribs
> who had been sitting at the fishing holes
> start in toward shore again,
> he set fire to the piles of branches.

He went around to wherever he had made a pile
and set it alight.

> They saw fires in many places on the hillside.

So they said,

> "It looks like the Yellowknives have come upon us."

During the night they got ready
and started to leave there before dawn.

When it became light,
they could be seen following one another on the lake.

Then the Yellowknife went down
to where the Dogribs had stayed.

When he got there, one campsite remained
but not a single person was left.

He saw that the Dogribs
had left their fishing platforms behind them.

The Yellowknife lived on their fish.
This is what they say.

[EPILOGUE]

Those were the last Dogribs who stayed around that place.
This is what they say.

They all ran downriver away from the Yellowknife.
The Yellowknife made all of the last of them run with his fires.
This is what they say.

Since then Dogribs haven't been seen anywhere on this land.
They all stay down the river where they ran.
This is what they say.

These days they call that place where they left
"Where people sit in a line."
It's where the Dogribs sat in a line at their fishing holes.

It was from there that the last Dogribs who were staying here
ran away from the Yellowknife.
This is what they say.

Li 1928: IX.19–24 / Li & Scollon 1976: 364–367

14 The Shaman of the Yellowknives

PROLOGUE]

There was a man called Sinew Water.

> He was a shaman.
> This is what they say.

> He dreamed about what was good
> and through his dreams he taught the people.
> He also told people about the future.
> He knew songs about the things which upset people
> and he was able to calm them down with those songs.

> Because of these things,
> people felt he was very useful.
> This is what they say.

[SCENE I]

One spring the people left the fort where they had been staying.

> A large group of them were crossing the great lake
> where the crossing was widest.
> There were many of them, women as well as children,
> crossing in many canoes.

> Besides the many large canoes,
> there were some men alone in small canoes.

When they had come into the middle of the lake,
it suddenly started to blow very hard.

> It still had not blown for long,
> but the waves had already started to swell.

> In time the waves began to swamp into the canoes.
> Women and children were bailing out the canoes,

but the water on the inside was rising nearly to the top,
and people were nearly drowning.

Suddenly the shaman called out to the people from behind.

He said,

> "Wait for me.
>   I'll go on ahead of you."

So they stopped to wait for him to pass by.

When he had passed by them
and pulled out in front of the first canoe,
he began to sing.

Immediately the wind stopped.
As soon as he began to sing,
it became calm.

And so in that way he paddled along ahead of the people,
      singing.

The people continued to cross along after him.

When they had come among the islands,
he led them to where a river flowed out.

He said,

> "We'll make camp here.
>   We'll put up on shore right here."

So everyone went up on the shore.

Then he spoke again,

> "Be careful when you put up the tepees.
>   Make them good and strong.
>   Also bring the canoes up on land.
>   The wind is not yet finished.
>   When it starts to blow again
>   it will be very strong.
>   Put some weights on the canoes.
>   Otherwise they might be blown away."

All of the tepees were put up quickly,
and all of the canoes were put up on land.

When the shaman saw that it was done, he said,

"Okay, let it blow now!
My children are all up on land."

Immediately it started to blow among the woods on the hilltop.
It roared like thunder.

And so the wind blew among the people.
The strong wind nearly blew the tepees apart.
It blew like that for a long time.
Then the wind became more moderate.

It continued to blow for three days.

Because of the way the shaman stopped the wind,
the people were not killed by the water.
This is what they say.

[SCENE II]

The shaman Sinew Water said,

"If I die,
there will not be a shaman here among the people.

"There is only one other person here who sees what I see.
Once, I met him.
He was rising as I was coming down.

"That other shaman said,

'I haven't seen any people around here until just now.
You're the first person I've seen.'

"Then he said,

'I'm a Beaver Indian.
What are your people?'

'I am a Yellowknife.'"

Then the Beaver Indian said to Sinew Water,

> "I am pleased that we have seen each other here.
> Let's not let our meeting be in vain.
> Let's give each other two songs."

So they gave each other two songs.
Sinew Water sang two songs.
The Beaver Indian himself also sang two songs,
a Beaver song and a Yellowknife song.

The Beaver Indian said,

> "Now I have seen a Yellowknife while I was rising.
> He gave me two songs."

This is what they say.

[SCENE III]

Once, Sinew Water was sick.

He spoke to his relatives,

> "My relatives,
> I am sick.
> But I am not sick with an illness.
> I am sick with the mind of the people.
> I will not be living,
> but you people will go on living.
>
> "I am told that
> if you say so, I will live.
> You are in control of it.
> I don't want to live here on the land
> after my children have died."

One of his relatives said,

> "We want you to go on living with us.
> Because of the way you speak to us,
> the children know what is right.
> You are very important to us."

Sinew Water said,

> "If only one person loves me,
> I cannot go on living.
> But I have been told that
> if many people think about one another,
> I will live."

At once all of his relatives told him,

> "Please go on living."

At once he revived.
He did not feel at all sick.
This is what they say.

[SCENE IV]

In that way he lived for a long time but finally became sick again.

Once again, he said to his relatives,

> "I have become an old man,
> but I am still alive here on the land.
> This is not pleasant for me,
> but I will go on living.

> "Again I am told that if you think about me
> I'll go on living."

But the people said nothing to him.

Thus he became very sick.

In the winter he said,

> "They have told me
> that when the leaves come out to a good size in the spring,
> then I will be called.
> I'll leave you at that time.
> Now I am living but
> I have also died already.

It doesn't matter if you urge me to live,
I will die."

In the spring when the leaves had grown to a good size,
he died quietly as if going to sleep.

This is what they say.

Li 1928: IX.41–53 / Li & Scollon 1976: 376–385

15 The Wise Man – Story One

Once, people were camped in a place.
This is what they say.

A man came back from hunting and said,

> "I have seen the tracks of our enemy.
>   They went across our tracks.
>   Judging from their tracks,
>   I'm sure it's a band of our enemy.
>
> "If they find us
>   they'll kill us.
>   There aren't many of us,
>   and it would be hard for us to defend against them."

There was a wise man living with them,
so someone said,

> "It would be good to tell the wise man about this."
>
>   So they went to the wise man.

They told him,

> "Enemy tracks have been seen."

This is what they say.

> "We thought we'd better tell you.
>   That's why we've come to you now."

The wise man asked them,

> "Who was it who saw the enemy tracks?"

One of the men said,

> "I'm the one who saw the tracks."

The wise man said,

> "Tell us exactly how it was
> when you saw the enemy tracks."

> So he told the wise man the story
> about how he'd seen the tracks.

> "There seem to be a lot of people."

For a long time the wise man didn't speak.

Suddenly he said,

> "When you were out hunting today,
> did you happen to see any places with open water?"

One of the men said,

> "I saw a place where there was open water."

The wise man said,

> "Okay, let's go there."

[SCENE II]

So they went there.

The wise man said,

> "Act as if you haven't seen anything.
> Go around enjoying yourselves like you usually do.

> "When we come to the place with open water,
> don't make any tracks.
> Just get together whatever ropes we have."

186

[SCENE III]

So that's how they came to the place with the open water.

> The water was frozen just a little on the surface
> but in the middle the ice was thin.

> When they got there, the wise man said,

>> "I'll go ahead of you.
>> You come along behind me.
>> Be careful to step only on my tracks
>> and come with one after the other.

>> "Two of you stay here with the ropes."

> So he started off carrying one end of the rope.

When the first rope came to its end,
the two men tied another rope to the end of it.

> By doing it that way
> he was able to walk all around the weak ice on strong ice.

> All of them followed him around on his tracks,
> and he came to a place
> which was directly across from the men.

> Then he said,

>> "Gather up spruce boughs for me."

> When they had gathered up a lot of spruce boughs
> they tied them to the middle section of the rope.

> Then he said to the men waiting across opposite him,

>> "Drag these spruce boughs across the ice."

> So they dragged the boughs across the ice,
> then the wise man dragged them back again toward himself.
> They dragged them back and forth like that many times.

> Finally they had made a wide trail right across,
> and the wise man pulled them back toward himself again.

He said,
  "Okay, that's enough."

He went on,

  "You two come around following our tracks.
  Come back here like that."

So the two men came around like he had said.

They had all come together.

The wise man said,

  "There's plenty of dry wood over here.
  Make shelters.
  We'll camp right here."

After the shelters were all built, he said,

  "All the children should play outside.
  Just act as though we don't know anything
    until it starts to get dark."

In the evening the children played and shouted together
    until it got dark.

Then the wise man said,

  "Okay, that's enough."

Then the wise man spoke to all of the people,

  "They'll probably only attack us early in the morning.

  "If the ice in the open water doesn't crack open,
  we'll defend ourselves.
  Even if the ice breaks,
    some of them will probably come out of the water.
  Kill anyone who comes out of the water."

So they pretended to go to sleep.
All the people sat through the night inside their shelters
    without fire.

[SCENE IV]

At dawn the next morning,
the ground started to thunder on the other side.

> The enemy had come to attack the people.

> They came running out onto the ice.
> They came running across the big trail
> made with spruce boughs.
> When they got to the middle of the trail,
> the newly formed ice broke through,
> and all of them fell into the water.

> Immediately the wise man said,

>> "The ice has broken through.
>> Get there as fast as you can."

> They all ran to the edge of the broken ice.

> The wise man said,

>> "Four of you get around to the other side.
>> Follow your own tracks."

> Four of them ran back around to the other side
>> on their own tracks.

The enemy was crawling up on top of each other,
each pushing the other down.

> Those who drowned drifted underneath the solid ice.

> In time there were very few of them left.

Finally not even one of them came out of the water.

> The enemy band had all been drowned.
> This is what they say.

[EPILOGUE]

The wise man said,

> "The water has killed a lot of people,
> but what will people say about it?
> We didn't order them to go there.
> It happened because they wished it on themselves.
> If we had ordered them to go out there
> we might have thought that we had killed them,
> but this isn't how it happened.

> "Now we didn't sleep at all last night.

> "Let's have a good sleep now in the daytime."

And he set out toward his home.

> The wise man acted this way
> and so he made the water kill the enemy.
> This is what they say.

Li 1928: x.5–18 / Li & Scollon 1976: 418–429

Mandeville's son, Philip Xavier Mandeville, commented that these two stories of the wise man were his father's favorites. Perhaps it is significant that these are the last two stories he told.

16 The Wise Man – Story Two

[PROLOGUE]

Once, a wise man was staying with the people.

[SCENE I]

A young man came back from hunting suddenly.

He said,

> "I've seen the enemy.
> I saw them a lot of them from the top of a hill."

Then another man came back.

He also said,

> "I passed near an enemy group.
> There were a lot of them.
> I saw them from the top of a hill
> but I don't think any of them saw me.

> "I ran from there as fast as I could."

So they all went to the wise man and told him about this.

He sat there thinking.

After a very long time he said,

> "Well, I was afraid all my thinking was in vain,
> but now I think maybe it isn't."

He asked,

> "When you were hunting did you see anywhere
> that a steep place goes down to a lake between hills?"

Two of them told him,

"There is a lake up ahead
where there is a steep place between hills."

He said,

"Okay, let's go there."

When they got there, he said,

"Make a trail
that goes from up there right down to the lake.

"Then when the snowshoe trail is made,
punch a hole in the ice at the base.

"When you've made a hole in the ice,
use all the kettles you have
and pour water down the trail.

"That way it'll freeze into ice."

When the water was well frozen, he said,

"Make it so that it runs right out on the ice."

When they had done that, he said,

"Pour more water on it again.
Make it very slippery right down to the lake."

They did as he said. Then he said,

"Make a tepee right in the middle.

"Just use four tepee poles."

When they were done with that, he said,

"Now you go ahead.

"I'll just say here."

But one of them said,

"It would be good if two of us stayed here with you.
If you sit here by yourself,
the enemy will probably kill you."

The wise man answered,

> "No. They'll just kill me.
> If I die, the two others will be killed too.
> So I'll just stay here by myself.
> I've lived for a long time already,
> so if the enemy kills me it means nothing.

> "It would be best for you young people to live.
> So if you travel a long way from here
> you'll come to somewhere that our people are camped.

> "If I live through this
> I'll follow along behind you.
> If I don't come,
> it'll be because I've been killed.
> I'll be gone."

So he put four green-wood clubs down by his side.

The others left him there.

[SCENE III]

Those who had left him there traveled day and night,
and by noon the next day came to the fish lake
where their relatives were staying.

> They told everybody what they knew.
> They explained what the wise man had done.

The people said,

> "The enemy will kill him.
> There are a lot of them.
> He's alone by himself,
> he can't possibly kill that many of them."

The people there said,

> "It would be best for us to go back to him.
> If the enemy kills him,
> they'll follow our trail here anyway."

So at once everyone started gathering together
    all of the arrows they had.

[SCENE IV]

By that evening they had reached a lake.

Suddenly they saw a man going along dragging something.
When they got to him
they saw that it was the wise man.

And they saw that what he was dragging along behind him
were all the bows he had taken from all the enemy he had killed.
This is what they say.

When he got to the people, he said,

"I have clubbed all of the enemy to death.
Here I've taken all of their bows.
I thought the orphans
who don't have any bows could use them.

"If you think you'd like to see what I did over there,
    go ahead.
I'll follow your tracks back to where the people are camped."

So he followed their tracks back to camp
while the others went on
to the place where he had killed the enemy.

When they got there,
what they saw was
people were lying dead
all along from the lake ice up to the tepee standing above.
They were lying there one against another all the way
        up to the tepee.

This is how the wise man killed so many people.

He stood in the tepee holding a green-wood club.

The people came to attack early in the morning.
They had seen that there was only one tepee up there,

so they thought that everybody was up there in that one tepee.
So they put on their snowshoes.

But it was still dark,
and they didn't see the ice.

So they went up, one after another, on the ice.
They kept falling and sliding downward.
They slid into the tepee.
The wise man was waiting there
and clubbed them on the head one after the other
with his big green-wood club.

[EPILOGUE]

So that's how they all slid downward to the lake, one after the other.

He clubbed down all the enemy band
even though he was alone by himself.
This is what they say.

Li 1928: X.19–32 / Li & Scollon 1976: 430–443

Dress from Fort Chipewyan, circa 1900

Part Two: Elicited Accounts

Campsite with birchbark freight canoe, Mackenzie River, circa 1910

17 Education

[PREFACE]

It's been said that our people didn't teach each other,
      but that isn't true.

    We have always taught each other.

Now I will tell you how people taught each other.

    The old men and old women taught the children.
    I'll tell you about that.

[PART I]

When an old man called for all the children,
they all came to him.

    Then he told the children about a long time in the past,
    about all of those who could do things well,
    those who had strong powers,
    those who were fast,
    or those who could hunt well and how they did that.

    He told the children stories about those capable people
    and about what they did that made them unlike others.

    It was thought that you should tell the children now
    about what people had done in the past.
    If they would act like those who were very capable,
    then these children could become like those earlier people.

    That's how the old man taught the children.

This is how a boy used to be taught to be a fast runner.

    They believed that if you dreamed of something which moved fast,
    then you yourself would be fast.

    They told him what to eat so he could become fast.

They also told him that if he ate certain things
he would not run fast.

Now I'll tell you what things keep people from running fast.

First of all, you should not eat hard meat.
You get heavy from that.

You shouldn't eat the flesh of unborn animals.
That soon makes your flesh weak.

Also, you should never eat jackfish intestines.
That makes your side ache when you run.

Never drink the water from the top of the snow.
That will make you heavy.

But if you only drink the water from soft surface snow,
that'll make you very light.

You should never go close to menstruating women.

You should be careful to not even step in their footsteps.
That takes your powers away.
If you've lost your powers,
when you think you can run fast
you wouldn't be able to do it.

The capability you get from your powers is only good
if they have not gone away.

Then he is taught what implements are used for hunting.

First, they make arrows for him.

They teach him how to use them to shoot things.

If he becomes capable at that,
they let him make arrows for himself.

They also tell him what kind of stick is used to make a bow.

They tell him how to make arrows with sticks
and what is good for bowstrings,
and also what feathers are used to feather the arrow.

Then they teach him how to hunt.

> They teach him what to use to make a fishnet,
> how it is made,
> and also how a snare is set.

> He is also taught all about snares:
> rabbit snares, lynx snares, bear snares,
> and also caribou snares and moose snares.

> They say how each one is used,
> with what materials it is made,
> and how it is set.

When he begins to hunt for game
he is taught how to hunt for moose.

> If he follows moose tracks
> he is also told how to do the tracking.

> He must note the wind direction.
> Also he has to see the thickets of trees.

> You only come up to a moose from downwind.
> That's because if one goes in the direction of the wind,
> the scent gives you away.

So then he teaches himself how to hunt through hunting.

> It isn't difficult to kill moose
> if you know how the moose acts,
> what it does when the wind blows,
> and what it does when the air is calm.

> You don't hunt for all the different kinds of game in the same way.
> Everybody teaches each other
> how to hunt for each different animal.

Then he is taught how to preserve his luck
when he handles the game animals he kills.

> He is told that if he handles game in a way
> that goes against the mind of the animal,
> it is unlucky for people.

They believe that he must do things correctly
so that he will not bring bad luck on himself.

Now one thing that is unlucky for people
is for a woman to eat from a moose head.

A woman should also be told
to be careful to avoid
walking over new meat.
It is also unlucky for people to step on meat.
People should be carefully warned of these things.

[PART II]

Now a young man would live as he had been taught.

If he did everything well according to his powers,
he would become lucky and capable of everything.
Because he could kill game better than anybody else
he could provide a living for the people staying with him.

Because of that many people would live with him.

Now the people who would live with him
all respect his mind and his action.

They would all work for him.

When everyone was spread out hunting,

if one of them saw tracks
he would not hunt for it himself.
He would tell the capable person.
If that one hunted for it
he would kill the game.
That would be well known,
so he would tell him.

The one who is capable would start to hunt for it the next day.

There would be no doubt that he would kill the animal.

When he went to hunt,
many people would follow him.

When he would kill something,
those who came to him would cut up the moose.

Some of them would make fires.

When the fires were made,
the meat would be roasted.

Everybody would eat well.

Then they'd make meat packs
for people to pack the meat home.

The capable man would not work himself.
He wouldn't pack even a little of it.

Now when they got home
they would put all the meat in the man's home.

They would roast the meat
and all eat together.

Then he would talk to everybody.

He would tell them how to work
and where to go hunting.

After he told them all of that,
they would go home.

Then before the night was over, a long time before dawn,

he would call out to the people.

"Why are you still sleeping?
Dawn came and you were still asleep.
Get up right away.
I'm already going hunting.
It's a long way to the moose tracks.
Hurry after me!"

Then he would go off hunting already.

Right away they would get up quickly
and start off after him.

Even if they traveled as quickly as they could,
he'd kill the moose before they got there.

When they would come to him,
he would be sitting by it.

Like before, some of them would cut up the moose.
Some of them would make a fire.

After the fire was made,
the meat would be roasted.

Again, after they ate,
they would make packs of meat
and pack off all the meat.

Nearly all the days would pass, one by one, in this way,
as they stayed with him.
This is what they say.

Li 1928: 1.1–23 / Li & Scollon 1976: 1, 2–17

18 About Fish

[PART I – FISHNETS]

This first part is about how fishnets were made.

The net was made with willow bark.
This is what they say.

You strip the willow bark in the spring before the bark gets loose.

Then the women twist this for the netting.

Then you weave the net.

Once again, they twist willow bark for the backing line.
After weaving the net, you put the backing on.

Then the fishnet floats are made.

Then you go get the sinkers.

The net is set from a canoe.

Even when the net is set,
you don't leave it for a long time.
It's never left for more than two days.
The willow bark will rot in the summer in warm water.

In the winter, though, the water is cold.

Even if you leave the net in the water for a long time,
it doesn't rot.
This is what they say.

[PART II – FISHHOOKS]

Now they didn't kill fish only with nets.
They also used fishhooks.

The line for the hook is made with willow bark.

The fishhook is made out of bone.

Hooks can also be made with eagle claws.

When the hook is made, you sew the bait on it.
Then you make a short stick.
You tie the line onto the fishhook
and sit at a fishing hole.

There you jig the stick up and down
until you catch a fish.
Sometimes there aren't any fish.
Sometimes when there are a lot of fish,
you don't have to sit at the fishing hole for long.
Even in a short time you catch a lot of fish.

Now you don't kill fish by just sitting there at the hole.

The hook would just lie on the bottom.

You have to hook the fish.

Years ago people lived on fish like that.
This is what they say.

[PART III – COOKING FISH]

Now this part is about how we cook fish.

Since people long ago didn't have kettles,
they could only roast fish.
This is what they say.

The fish is cut into two pieces of equal size.

You hang it on a stick in front of a fire.

Now it roasts while it is hanging there.

When one side is roasted, you turn it around.
Then the other side roasts.
To keep it from getting ashes on it from the fire,
you put something under it.
Sometimes it'll fall before it is entirely cooked.

For some fish, you first cut it open
and thoroughly clean out the insides.

    Then you make a cut in the tail.
    You tie a string there and hang it in front of the fire to roast.

You turn it while it is roasting
to keep it from being burned on one side.

    In that way it won't get burned.
    Even if it is a strong fire,
    it will be well cooked.

[PART IV – COOKING TROUT]

Now this is about how you cook trout.

Sometimes you eat the insides of the trout raw.

Just at the time of summer when the leaves are growing out,

    you can catch a big fat trout and cut it open.
    You cut it carefully into two connected halves.

    Then you put leaves on a big, hot fire.

    Then you throw the trout into the fire.

    You turn it constantly with a poker.

    You take it out when it is fully browned.

Then you shout, drawing it out,

    "I have cut the riiiib boooones!"

Well, right then anybody who hears you comes running.

Now the one who has cooked the fish starts eating
        as soon as he's shouted that out.

    He has called everybody,
    but he doesn't wait for them to eat.

    Everybody eats it up as quickly as they can.

That's how they eat.

They might not have eaten it all and somebody comes.

He starts to eat immediately as well.

Anybody who comes after that also does the same.
Many people eat as quickly as they can
until the trout is entirely eaten up.
In that way the trout is completely eaten
even if it is very large.

Of course sometimes someone comes
after the trout has been completely eaten.

Even though he ran hard
he doesn't get even a taste.
That's how he goes home again.

Well, they really laugh at him.

But they don't really say anything to him.
That's just all in fun.

They really enjoy that,
so they do it sometimes.

People think this is really a feast.

It makes you happy just to think about it.

Li 1928: 1.24–36 / Li & Scollon 1976: 2, 18–27

19 How I Made a Canoe

Once, I made a canoe.

I started by working hard to get the material for the canoe.

First of all I peeled the birchbark from the upper part of a tree,
and I collected all the wood for the canoe.
I chopped one tree down for the canoe ribs,
but even though that tree should have split straight,
it did not split well.
So I felled another big tree
and split the canoe ribs from that tree.
I also got some other parts of the canoe from it.

After I made all the parts of the canoe
I made a place on the ground to lay out the canoe.

I put rocks on the spread-out birchbark.
A canoe made with warped birchbark is not good,
so I only use well-stretched birchbark to make canoes.
So I spread the birchbark on the ground which I had leveled.
I laid logs on it
and then rocks on that.

To make sure that the birchbark would be stiff and flat,
I pulled up all the roots.
I also tore them all apart.
That's how I put the bottom of the canoe down.

When I had cut the bottom out,
a woman sewed up the bark for me.
I laid the birchbark down for the sides of the canoe
and fastened it well with wooden nails.

When that was done,
the woman sewed the sides for me.
I put the gunwale on
and also trimmed the sides above the gunwale.
The woman sewed the bow posts down for me.
Then I put the inside keel in the canoe.

I put the small endpieces on the keel,
and the props for the bow posts.

I had made the keel much too long,
so I cut a part of it off to the correct length.

Then I put the frame in the canoe.
I put the ribs in the canoe,
fitting them to each other.

Then I spread hot water all over it.

That heated the birchbark throughout.
I carefully tapped the ribs into place,
one after another.

In that way I adjusted them
finally into their proper place.

That made the birchbark stretch quite tight on the frame
of the canoe.

Then I went to look for pitch.
I knocked the pitch down from the tree
and brought it home in a sack,
and I boiled it.

As the pitch was boiling,
I crumbled charcoal into it.

That made it black.
Then the woman put the pitch on the canoe for me.
So I made a paddle for myself
and paddled around in the new canoe.

It was new, so there was no water in it.

It also moved fast.
I had made every part of the canoe frame thin,
so the canoe was light.
I made only the thwarts strong
in order to carry the canoe around by them.
If they were not strong,
and I got up quickly in the canoe,
my weight would break the thwart.
When the thwart is strong there is no danger of that.

[EPILOGUE]

I finished making a good canoe.

Because I made one small rib short,
there was one place that was not tight.
But that was not a serious fault.

I used that canoe for a long time.

Li 1928: IX.25–32 / Li & Scollon 1976: not published.
First published as Li Fang-kuei 1964: "A Chipewyan Ethnological Text,"
International Journal of American Linguistics 30(2): 132–136.

20 How I Tanned a Moose Hide

[PART I]

Once, I shot a moose.

It collapsed on its front side.

It was so big that it was hard work to turn it facing upward.

I severed its head
and then I cut it down the front.

Once I had cut down the front side,
I cut the legs open.
Then I tore the skin off the legs
and the skin from the body.
I removed the legs
and then gutted it.
I cleaned out the entire body cavity.

I used an axe to chop the ribs off
and also to chop the back into two pieces.
When I had gathered all the meat together
I cached it.

I brought home just the moose hide.

[PART II]

I prepared a place to tan the moose hide by making a frame for it.

With the tanning frame made,
I used a rope to stretch out the moose hide on the frame.

Then I scraped the inner side of the hide,
carefully picking off all of the fibers.
Then I suspended the hide in the frame on a forked stick.

I left it like that for a while.

Once the inside had dried,
I took the hide and frame back down.

Then I scraped the outside of the hide.

When it was scraped clean,
I untied the moose hide from the frame.

Then I put the hide up over a smoking fire
in order to smoke it thoroughly inside.

I kept turning it over above the smoke,
so the smoke got into it quickly,
and then I rubbed it all over with brains.

So it would get more completely smoked,
I put it up over the smoke again.

Before too long
I took it back down,
and I put it in water to tan it.

When it was thoroughly soaked,
I took it out of the water.

Then I wrung it out with a twisting pole.
I wrung it very hard,
but there was still some water dripping out of it,
so I tied one end of the twister to a tree.

I left the twisted hide that way for a long while.
Then I twisted it a little again,
but no water dripped out.
So I took the hide down.

Then I stretched and pulled it in all directions over the fire.

For a long time I turned it over the fire.
Sometimes I stretched it,
and then again I put it back over the fire,
then stretched it again.

At last the hide was dry.

[PART III]

I thought I had made it very soft, so I folded it up and stored it.

[PART IV]

Three days later I took the hide out
because I wanted to smoke the inner side.

> I thought I had made it soft,
> but because it wasn't thoroughly dry,
> I discovered that it had stiffened when it dried.

> It was too stiff to make moccasins with,
> so I put it back into water.
> When it was thoroughly soaked,
> I took it out and twisted it again.

> Then I repeated what I did in the first place.
> I kept on stretching it
> until it became thoroughly dried.

> When it was quite soft,
> I stored it again,
> wondering what might become of it.

> I left it there for a long time,
> but it didn't become stiff.

> So I sewed it into a the shape of a sack
> and smoked the inner side with wood punk.

That's how I tanned a moose hide well.

Li 1928: IX.33–40 / Li & Scollon 1976: 16, 368–375

21 How I Hunted Beaver

[PROLOGUE]

One winter we camped near beavers.

[PART I]

There was a large beaver lodge which we tore down.

Then we dug through the ice
to form a trench on the shore to look for beavers.
I dug where there seemed to be a beaver den.
I poked around there with a curved stick,
one place after another.
It was deep in the center so that I couldn't reach bottom.
So I dug through the ice down to the bottom of the lake.

Bubbles from the beavers started to rise up from underwater.
I dug through the ice toward the land.
Then I took some sticks
to make a good barrier across.

When there were no gaps in the barrier,
I said to the others with me,

"I've barred the beaver den.
  Let's see now what happens
  when one of us digs through the beaver den."

So everybody gathered around me.
When I had thrown the loose chunks of ice
        out of the hole in the ice,
I put two willow sticks into the beaver trail.

I took a beaver hook with me to the barrier
and shoved the hook underwater in the ice hole.
One man who was poking above the beaver den
suddenly broke through.

Immediately the beavers crawled into the water,
and the water roiled.

Right then the two willow sticks which were stuck in the water
began to shake.

I tried to hook the beaver in the water quickly,
and I got one.
I pulled it out of the water
and threw it to one side in the snow.

Right away I pushed the hook into the water again.
Again the water became turbulent
and I hooked another beaver.

I threw it into the snow,
and the other people there clubbed them to death.

The water became still.

We dug a big hole above the beaver den,
but only two beavers had crawled into the den there,
so we only killed these two.
One of them was a medium-sized beaver,
and the other was a large one.

There must have been a lot of beavers.
They were over by the lake.
So we separated from each other
and searched for the beaver den.
I dug in the ice time and again,
and I poked around in several places,
but I didn't find the beaver den.

Finally, not far from where I'd taken the two beavers out,
I poked through the ice.
That's where the beaver den was reaching up to the shore.
So I poked holes across the ice
and made a good barrier.
Then I called everybody back to me.

When they had come back,
one of them dug through above the beaver den for me.

Suddenly the beavers dove into the water.
The water became agitated.
While I was shoving the beaver hook into the water
and standing by the ice hole with the two willow sticks,
the sticks shook again.

Quickly I hooked at it again
but I missed it.
So I hooked another beaver which had crawled into the water
and threw it aside into the snow.

I realized that it was a small beaver.

I stood there by the barrier, shoving my hook into the water,
but the water didn't move.

Many chunks of ice fell into the hole,
so I scooped them out with a wooden paddle.
But still the water didn't move.

At first the water had moved a lot when the beavers dove under.
Just one beaver wouldn't cause such turbulence.
If the beaver trail went away in opposite directions,
then the beavers must have gone the other way.
I thought,

"I'll look carefully at this."

Where they had dug through before at the beaver den,
I dug it further to enlarge it.

Then I saw the beaver den.
The beavers had crawled way back in the beaver den
to avoid the danger.
I saw three beavers sitting there.

I dug through the ground above them.
We made it a big hole.

We pulled the small beavers out by their tails.
It was hard to pull the larger beavers out by the tails,
because their feet clung to the ground.

Finally we lifted up the hind part
so that its back feet couldn't grasp the ground.
We pulled at them,
and since they couldn't hold the ground,
we were able to take them out.

Now we had killed five beavers altogether.

Apparently there were a lot of beavers
living with these medium-sized beavers.
The beaver lodge was very large.
It was splendid.
They had lots of food stored up.
From the wood they were working on,
that was lying around on the ground,
it was clear that there were many of them.

So we all said,

   "Let's keep searching for them."

So we kept on searching for the den.

Finally evening came.

We camped there by the shore of the beaver lake.

In the evening we gutted all of the beavers.

We examined the female beaver's womb.
That told us that we'd killed almost all of the beavers.
Just one medium-sized beaver
and one young beaver were still alive.

In the morning we looked for beavers again.

We had not yet found their den,
so we ate around noon.

Somebody said,

   "They must be somewhere
   at the beaver dam."

Someone else said,

"There was a small beaver lodge somewhere on the bog,
but we didn't see it because there was too much snow.
That must be the reason."

They said,

"Let's give up and go home now.
If one of us here sees it again next winter
he can kill the beavers for himself.
It is a medium-sized beaver now,
so by spring it may have young ones.
Next winter there may be a family of beavers here.

Even if one of us here doesn't see it,
if someone else kills them,
it'll be useful to him."

So we left there and came back home.

[PART II]

Then someone said,

"Let's go out and look for caribou."

So the next day we started looking for caribou.

After we had traveled for some time
we found a lot of old caribou tracks on a lake.
There were also a lot of faint old caribou tracks in the woods.
But we didn't see any fresh tracks.

We decided to make our camp there.

Early the next morning we started off again.
We climbed up onto a hilltop facing the lake.
From there we saw that there were many caribou
lying down on the lake.
So we started down the valley toward the lake.

A small creek flowed into that valley out of the mountain.
The ice buildup from that creek extended up the mountain.

The water in the creek was still flowing
because it came out of a spring from inside the mountain.

The spring water was forming a glacier up in the mountain.

Glaciers were in several places some distance into the woods.
There were a lot of caribou tracks around those glaciers.

Because it was a big lake,
we surrounded the caribou.
We made trail marks in the bay.
One person sat at the end of each point of land in the bay.
We made trail marks like that all around the lake.

When we had finished,
one of us ran toward the caribou.
While he was running around shooting at the fleeing caribou,
each person sitting at a point of land in the bay
shot at those which ran near his point.

The caribou scattered and fled in every direction.

That is how we killed nearly all of them.
Not many escaped from the shooting.
In the end they ran over the trail marks.

They finally ran away from the lake onto the shore.
We killed many different kinds of caribou:
fat females without young ones,
fat males which were both big and small,
young three-year-old males,
females with their young,
and two male one-year-olds.

[PART III]

At spring breakup I started out in a canoe to hunt beaver.

I paddled up against the swift current in the river.
There I reached an eddy below a point in the bay.
I just floated in that position.

Suddenly a beaver swam into view
at the point of the bay.
It was swimming toward me.
I shot it,
put it in the canoe,
and started paddling again.

I went a long way upstream,
where I saw beaver tracks.
There were beaver logs lying around.

I paddled quietly against the current
until I saw a beaver sitting in shallow water.
So I paddled toward it.

While I was still at some distance,
it caught my scent
and dove underwater out in the river.
I drifted with the current looking for it.
There was something floating from the shore
into the lake down below in the bay.
I thought,

    "That's where it will come out."

So while I was floating toward that place,
it poked its head up in front of me,
under the things which were floating out onto the lake.
When I floated close enough
I shot it in the head.

Quickly I thrust the beaver spear into it.
It drowned while I was holding it underwater with the spear.

I paddled up to the shore
and put the beaver into the canoe.

Then I started paddling upriver again.

I had gone a long way
when darkness came in the evening.
It was too dark to sight along the barrel of my rifle.

I went out onto the shore.

After camping there that night,
early at the next dawn
I started off paddling again.

At sunrise
a beaver was swimming toward me from along the shore upstream.
I sat and waited for it.
It swam near me,
and I shot it in the head.
But I didn't shoot it well.
It was stunned
so it did not dive.
It just swam around and around,
so I paddled around after it.

Finally I caught up to it
and shot it in the head again.

It floated up and I put it in the canoe.
Then I started off again.

I had not gone far
when an otter swam toward me.

While it was still at some distance
it caught my scent and dove.

Even though I paddled around for a long time
I didn't see it again.

In this way I had paddled far up the river.
I stopped to sleep while it was still daytime.

After I had slept
I skinned the beavers.
I stretched them flat
after I had carefully cut the flesh from the skin.
Then I laid the beaver skins in their stick frames on a big spruce
          with many branches.

I set out again still upstream.

Even though I went a long way
I didn't see any beaver tracks,
so when evening came I slept there.

Early the next morning
I started back downstream.
When I came back to where I had laid out the beaver skins
I picked them up again.

The skins had dried out nicely while I was away,
so I took out all the sticks
with which I had stretched the skins.

I folded the skins carefully.

I put the skins into the canoe.

Again I set out downstream.
With the strong current
I arrived home that evening.
Just as I came near home,
a beaver came swimming toward me.
I shot it.

That's how I came home.

Li 1928: IX.54–X.4 / Li & Scollon 1976: 18, 386–417

François Mandeville with a Hudson's Bay Company pelt press, Fort
Resolution, circa 1905

Part Three: Commentary

The house that François Mandeville built in the early 1920s at Fort Chipewyan, and the nearby Athabasca Café, photographed in 1976

The Narrative Ethnography
of François Mandeville

In story 10, "The Adventures of Beaulieu," Mandeville says,

At first there were only two Métis staying around here.

This is what they say.

> *Their French fathers came to this land by canoe.*
> *Two Métis came out of their marriages to Indian women.*
> *One of them was called Beaulieu,*
> *and the other was called Mandeville.*

> *The one called Beaulieu had strong powers.*
> *All of the people were afraid of him.*

He makes no further mention of his own heritage, the Mandeville heritage. In an interview in 1977, Mandeville's son, Philip Xavier, told me that his father, François, was born in 1878, and that his father's father was Michel Mandeville. Philip said that his grandfather Michel had been an interpreter for the Treaty Eight Commission in 1899. Thus François Mandeville was the son of a Métis interpreter.

Most of what I know about the chronology of François Mandeville's life comes from that same interview with Philip in 1977. In summary:

1878 · *Born at Fort Resolution, Northwest Territories, Canada.*
1901 · *Marriage (at Fort Rae on Great Slave Lake) to Margaret Lafferty of Fort Rae.*
1902 · *Son, Philip Xavier Mandeville, born.*
1908 · *Moved to Hay River where he worked for the Hislop & Nagle trading company.*

1910 · *Moved to Fort Providence at the outlet of Great Slave Lake into the Mackenzie River. In that year his father, Michel Mandeville, died. François returned to Fort Resolution and began work for the Hudson's Bay Company because this was his father's wish.*

1911 · *Moved to Fort Smith to manage the Hudson's Bay Company there.*

1913 · *Moved to Fort Wrigley down the Mackenzie to manage the Hudson's Bay Company there.*

1915 · *Moved much farther down the river to Arctic Red River, also as manager for the Hudson's Bay Company.*

1917 · *Moved back to Fort Rae for the Hudson's Bay Company. After moving there, he became ill. He underwent surgery but was still unable to return to work.*

1921 · *Moved to Fort Chipewyan, but then worked at times at Fond du Lac, Saskatchewan (at the other end of the lake), for Hamden Nalley.*

1925 · *Returned to stay at Fort Chipewyan. Made boats, skiffs, canoes, and trapped for furs.*

1928 · *Worked with Li Fang-kuei for six weeks of the summer.*

1940· *Returned to working for the Hudson's Bay Company and went to Jackfish River (on the Peace River) to trade for them.*

[later 1940s] · *Returned to Fort Chipewyan.*

1952 · *Died at Fort Chipewyan, 74 years of age.*

François Mandeville came down to Fort Chipewyan from the Great Slave Lake and Mackenzie River areas where he had spent much of his life because he had done well with the Hudson's Bay Company. He was not well at that time, and his sister, who had married into the Mercredi family, was there. It was known to be a good place for hunting and fishing.

He built a house at Fort Chipewyan, next to the Athabasca Café and across the road from the Hudson's Bay Company. Mandeville and Li Fang-kuei met for their work at this house. Philip – who at that time was 25 years of age, exactly the same as Li – said that while they worked downstairs, he lay quietly upstairs all day and listened.

Although Mandeville had not dictated stories in this way before, he was the son of an interpreter and he himself had become an interpreter for the court. According to Philip, he was able to dictate stories very slowly and carefully, making sure that he got everything just right. Philip also remembered that they did not stay at the house all the time. They sometimes went out to visit people staying in tents around the settlement.

While it is difficult to imagine how they could have found the time in the face of what they accomplished in these quick six weeks, it was on one of these breaks from the dictation when Li recorded story 4, "His Grandmother Raised Him," as told by Baptiste Forcier. Philip commented that Forcier was an 'old, old man' at that time. Li once mentioned to me that Mandeville felt that Forcier was very much the superior storyteller and had arranged for Li to make this transcription. Of course Li would also have wanted to assess the kinds and scope of linguistic variability within the community, and these visits in the company of Mandeville would have been his way of doing that.

The language of the home for Mandeville and his wife was French. In addition to English and Chipewyan, he was also competent in Slavey, Dogrib, and Hare. Philip says that while he was at Arctic Red River he also learned to speak Gwich'in.

Li Fang-kuei was directed to François Mandeville because he asked for an interpreter, and everyone knew Mandeville as the best there was. While the slow dictation style of their work was different from the way Mandeville usually told the stories, Philip did not feel that the stories were substantially different in any way. Of course he had heard the often-told spoken versions as well as these slow, careful dictations. He believed that Mandeville would not have forgotten anything in the process of slow dictation.

François Mandeville learned the ABC's, as Philip put it, from an Oblate priest, Father Louis Dupire. He had beautiful handwriting. This leads to an important point about literacy. His son commented that his father was a religious man and often read the Bible in syllabics, an orthography originally designed for writing Cree, which had been modified for use in Athabaskan liturgical materials as well as for the Bible. Philip commented that his father was very interested in Li's work because he was dissatisfied with the English and French alphabetic orthographies as well as Chipewyan syllabics, which he rightly considered inadequate to represent the complex phonologies of Athabaskan languages. Li had what he wanted, and he studied Li's writing system as assiduously as Li studied Mandeville's phonology, morphology, and syntax.

Philip told me that Mandeville read a great deal. He also said that Mandeville's main way of learning was to stand by the woodstove in his various stores and trade stories with the old people who came in. About Mandeville it was said, 'He could talk on any subject with the best of them.'

After hearing many tellings of his father's stories as well as the stories of many others over the years, Philip held the view that each storyteller has a different version of a given story, but that each person would have only one of them. As he said, 'That's the story and that's it: That's the way it goes on right now. A different person tells it and it's all out of shape.'

WHO WAS LI FANG-KUEI?

Li Fang-kuei (李方桂) was a precocious young linguist in 1928 when he went to Fort Chipewyan. He had just finished his Ph.D. at the University of Chicago under Edward Sapir but had also studied there with Leonard Bloomfield. The Chicago doctorate was his third university degree in as many years. He was 25 years old.

Li had arrived at the University of Michigan from China in 1924. At that point he could read and write in English but had no experience speaking the language. In just a little more than a year he completed a B.A. degree. His teachers were justifiably impressed with him and arranged for him to continue his studies at Chicago with Sapir and Bloomfield. More details of his education at Chicago have been recorded (Scollon & Scollon 1979; Yue-Hashimoto 2000/2001), but a summary will be sufficient here.

In two years, between arriving in Chicago in 1926 and going to Fort Chipewyan in 1928, he completed both his M.A. and his Ph.D. In that short time he had studied some 18 different languages, five of them in the Athabaskan language family. Seven of the languages he studied were ones on which he had done primary fieldwork, collecting stories or other material through phonetic dictation. Despite this breadth of linguistic knowledge, the University of Chicago delayed granting his Ph.D. by a few months because he had neglected to take the required reading exams in French and German. These he completed without any problem.

Li Fang-kuei's primary interests were the languages of China, Tibet, and Thailand. He had come to America because he had heard of the new methods which had been developed by the Americans to study the history of unwritten languages through the comparison of contemporary dialects. This historical-comparative method had been established in the study of Indo-European languages, and Edward Sapir and Leonard Bloomfield were leading pioneers in its use in the study of unwritten languages.

During that period at Chicago, Sapir and Bloomfield both taught Indo-European and American languages in alternating years. When Li Fang-kuei studied with Edward Sapir in the academic year 1927–28, it was Sapir's year to teach American languages through the study of Athabaskan. That year Bloomfield was teaching Indo-European. Li took just the one course with Sapir, an 'introduction to language' course which was the vehicle both Sapir and Bloomfield used to teach their new historical-comparative methodology.

Most of Li's education in this methodology was developed outside of class. One evening, for example, Sapir took him along while he did fieldwork on Navajo in a Chicago home. Sapir just told Li to take notes. He himself conducted his business as usual but without letting Li see what notes he was taking. Afterward, he let Li compare their notes.

Impressed with Li's abilities on the basis of such notes, Sapir gave Li his field notes from a summer's work on Sarcee. His instructions, according to what Li told me, were to 'see what he could do with them.' Li worked on them for a few weeks, using Sapir's other work as a model, and produced a paper. That paper was accepted as Li's master's thesis and published in 1931 in the *International Journal of American Linguistics.*

The following summer Sapir initiated Li into real fieldwork by taking him to California. Again, Sapir allowed Li to accompany him when he worked on Hupa, letting him take independent notes and then compare them with those of his teacher. Now, however, he even allowed Li to ask a question or two. After a week Sapir sent Li off to work on his own on Mattole and whatever other languages he could find. Li's grammar of Mattole was accepted as his doctoral dissertation that fall.

Four decades later, in Honolulu, I took one course from Li Fang-kuei: a seminar in Athabaskan linguistics. Bill Seaburg and Geoffrey Nathan were my classmates. I had just completed my own first fieldwork on Athabaskan at Arctic Village, Alaska, in the summer of 1972. The language there is Gwich'in. Edward Sapir had done his fieldwork on Gwich'in with John Fredson from Venetie at a vocational school which Fredson was attending in the eastern USA. He had passed his Gwich'in notes on to Li. In the first half of the course Li lectured on historical-comparative Athabaskan. He enjoyed using examples from Gwich'in which came from Sapir's notes. In almost every case his memory of the correct Gwich'in forms learned from Sapir's notes when he'd first studied them in 1927–28, more than forty years earlier, was quicker than mine, though I had been in the field with native speakers only a few weeks earlier.

In the second half of the course we began the study of a specific text in Chipewyan. It was Mandeville's story 19, "How I Made a Canoe." Li began this section of the course by simply speaking the title. He looked at us and, with a gesture, indicated that we should repeat after him. We struggled to do that and then, a phrase at a time, he led us through an oral recitation of the first paragraph of the story. He discouraged us from looking at the printed text while we did this.

Then he told us to go home and memorize the story before the next class. He said it was important for us to have the story 'in our ears' before we began our close linguistic analysis. We then worked through the story word by word, morpheme by morpheme, trying to recapitulate Li's explanation for each syllable and each word. A few weeks later he then gave us story 21, "How I Hunted Beaver," which we had never seen before. He had written it out phonemically by hand from his original notes. His instructions were: 'Do the same thing on your own.' In each subsequent class he checked our analyses against each other's and against his own.

When the course was finished, I received the grade of A-minus. As far as we know, he never gave a higher grade. He then gave me the ten notebooks of Chipewyan stories from 1928 along with his boxes of some

2,800 file slips. He simply said, 'See what you can do with these.' This was entirely outside of the formal structure of my doctoral program. First I prepared a typescript of all of the file slips exactly as he had written them in the field, in phonetic transcription complete with overwritten corrections. Then I made a typescript of the texts, regularizing the phonology as we had analyzed it in the seminar, starting from Li's own phonological retranscription of "How I Hunted Beaver." Finally I prepared a facing-page translation of the texts. I finished the project two years later in 1975 and gave it to him. Li said nothing at the time but arranged to have the book, *Chipewyan Texts,* published by the Academia Sinica in Taipei (Li & Scollon 1976).

After the book was published, Li called me into his office so he could give me a copy. The air was blue with the smoke of his cigar as he reached down and pulled out a fragile typescript which had been tied up with ribbon almost 50 years before. It was his own phonological analysis and translation which he had made in 1929 and then had typed while he was in Berlin. He had never mentioned that this work existed. He told me to compare them. They were substantially the same.

After his early Athabaskan work, Li's career had focused chiefly on the historical reconstruction of Archaic Chinese and Tai. (Tai is the name of the language family to which Thai, Lao, and several dozen other southeast Asian languages belong.) When Li returned from Fort Chipewyan in 1928, Sapir arranged a Rockefeller grant for him to return to China to do fieldwork there. In 1930, however, Li no longer needed the grant, as he was chosen to be a member of the prestigious Institute of History and Philology of the Academia Sinica in Beijing, along with his lifetime friend the linguist Chao Yuen Ren (趙元任). He continued doing fieldwork in China throughout the war, dodging soldiers and refugees as he moved from village to village, collecting priceless primary data on many languages. Also during this period he published his study of Chipewyan consonants with the Academia Sinica (Li 1933a) as well as his study of Chipewyan verb stems in the *International Journal of American Linguistics* (Li 1933b).

Sapir arranged a position at Yale for Li, which he took up in 1938. Unfortunately, Sapir passed away in 1939. Li told me that he felt that at that time he would not do well in the United States without the protection of his mentor. As a result, Li returned to China. I suspect as well that Li's first love was linguistic fieldwork and that he really preferred doing fieldwork in China to a life of academic prestige at Yale. In any event, in 1939 he left the position that might have established his reputation as one of the key figures in American linguistics.

When the new government of the Communist Party came to power in 1949, the Institute of History and Philology moved to Taiwan. So did Li and his family, but he was there only briefly. He accepted a position at the University of Washington in 1949. Although he is remembered now for his foundational work in Chinese, Tibetan, and Tai linguistics, during most of his long stay at Washington, he taught language courses, not courses in linguistics. This work simply relied on his abilities as a native speaker of Chinese, not on his analytical knowledge and skills. His twenty years there did not even provide him with meaningful retirement benefits, but through the efforts of Laurence C. Thompson and Byron Bender, the University of Hawai'i offered Li the status of Professor Emeritus, with the needed support for his retirement. Thus he moved to Hawai'i in 1969 and was finally able to teach a few courses based on his lifetime of fieldwork and linguistic analysis.

When I studied with him at the University of Hawai'i at the end of his career, Li Fang-kuei was the only linguist whose work was considered foundational in three separate language families: Na-Dené (which includes Athabaskan), Chinese, and Tai. And that was the only time in his long career as a linguist that he taught Athabaskan.

Edward Sapir had a reason, back in 1928, for sending his brilliant young student to Fort Chipewyan. At that time the use of phonemic tone in Athabaskan languages was poorly understood. Sapir felt that a Chinese linguist who already spoke two modern Chinese languages – Mandarin and Cantonese – would be perfectly suited to understand the way in which tone worked in Northern Athabaskan languages. Among linguists themselves, the content of the stories which they collected were generally felt to be of little intrinsic interest. Stories were merely a way to get words spoken in a meaningful context. From that point of view the centerpiece of the work was not the stories but the 2,800 file slips of lexical notes which Li brought back from his summer's work.

Li arrived at Fort Chipewyan in late June. He worked with Mandeville for six weeks, ending in early August. Then, inviting Mandeville to join him, he went downriver to Fort Smith in the Northwest Territories. Li told me that by the time they went down to Fort Smith, Mandeville had grown tired. They were at Fort Smith for about a week. After they did a little fieldwork there, Li went by himself farther down the Mackenzie to Fort Good Hope, where he collected several stories and file slips of lexical notes in Hare before the summer was over and he returned to Chicago. A small man to begin with, Li commented that he had lost twenty pounds in the course of the summer's work.

THE COLLABORATION OF LI AND MANDEVILLE

For about six weeks Li and Mandeville met in Mandeville's house to work eight hours a day for six days of the week. Each had aims of his own. Li wanted to get enough material for linguistic analysis so that he could produce a relatively exhaustive description of the Chipewyan language with a special focus on tone. Mandeville had at least two goals. One was to learn to write Chipewyan – and of course other languages – using Li's phonetic-phonemic orthography. His other goal, the one with which this book is concerned, was to use the occasion to make a comprehensive collection of the best Chipewyan stories. Li's many publications on Chipewyan and Athabaskan make it clear that he achieved his goal. The stories in this book make it clear that Mandeville also achieved his goal of creating a narrative ethnography of the Chipewyan people.

In the course of the six weeks together they produced ten notebooks of stories. All the stories are included here. (Several notebook pages are also photographically reproduced in the appendix, page 265.) The notebook entries were made in two stages. In the first stage, Li recorded Mandeville's narration as quickly as possible given the constraints of dictation. This is the upper line of the transcription, in Chipewyan. At the conclusion of each story, they returned to the beginning. Li read the transcription in Chipewyan a few words at a time, giving Mandeville the opportunity to make corrections.

Then Li queried each word, first to make a word-by-word translation into English. Mandeville gave these word translations in either French or English. Li recorded only the English result of what was sometimes a double translation – Chipewyan to French, French to English.

But in addition to the simple word-by-word translations, they worked to get the fullest paradigmatic sets they could achieve for each word. In practical terms they focused on verb stems. For example, for the verb translated in story 11 as 'he became [a wolf],' Li asked for, and Mandeville supplied, the forms 'I became a wolf,' 'you became a wolf,' 'we became wolves,' and so forth. Li also recorded such forms as 'he is becoming a wolf,' 'he will become a wolf.' Li wrote these paradigms on 4″ × 6″ sheets. These are the 2,800 slips I have mentioned. The two men considered a story completed only when the file slips as well as the two strands of text in the notebook were finished.

There are two points about how they worked which are important. First of all, their eight-hour workday includes only the time they spent together. After they finished each day together, according to Philip Mandeville, his father spent a few hours going over what he had learned about writing, carefully practicing writing things out in Chipewyan. There is little doubt that he was also preparing himself for the next dictation.

Li also continued to work after their eight-hour sessions. In his case he spent his time sorting and cross-referencing his rapidly growing file of lexical notes. These notes are cross-referenced to each other as well as to the place in the story where the question first arose. There is surprisingly little duplication of notes across the six weeks. This can only mean that Li was quite aware of which words had been used before and for which he had already taken notes. No doubt Mandeville was also much involved in this process of expanding the stories paradigmatically, because the notes became more complex with more developed paradigms as the work went on.

But that is the first point: They were both working very hard at their separate tasks. The second point is that Mandeville was paying close attention to the actual stories he was telling, particularly to the narrative structure of the stories. In the written transcriptions we see in the ten notebooks, there are relatively few corrections of words or of syntactic structure. What we see instead is careful correction of discourse markers, words which are often translated as 'then,' 'after that,' or sometimes just 'well.' (For more on these, see Scollon 1977.) By manipulating these markers, Mandeville in some cases elevated a section of the story to greater prominence. In other cases he demoted a main section into a subsection of another episode. It is this care, taken by both Mandeville and Li, that underlies the typography or print-structure of the stories as presented in this book. Mandeville's choice of marker is what determines how any given line or verse is presented. I am quite confident that what was written in the notebooks was what Mandeville wanted written there.

There is one further important indication of the coherence of this collection of stories. In 1976 when my wife and I did our own fieldwork at Fort Chipewyan, we had taken along with us the book of stories published as *Chipewyan Texts* (Li & Scollon 1976). We had many occasions to show the book to people and to read portions of the book to them. One of the stories, "His Grandmother Raised Him" (story 4), was not told by Mandeville. Mandeville had asked Baptiste Forcier to tell the story and had taken Li to him for the dictation and transcription. Li and I omitted this story from *Chipewyan Texts* (1976) for two reasons. The first was that we wanted the collection to be just the stories told by Mandeville. The other was that to my naïve eyes, Forcier's story seemed of lesser quality, both as linguistic material and as narrative art, than the others in the collection.

We were quickly set straight on this matter at Fort Chipewyan. People were keen to know which stories were in the book. There was a general agreement that 'old François' (or 'our grandfather') had put together an excellent collection, but everyone was puzzled that "His Grandmother Raised Him" was not in the book. 'Damned funny old François didn't tell that one.' It was a gap spotted by everyone.

When we explained that Mandeville had actually arranged for the story to be told to Li by Baptiste Forcier, we learned something more. Yes, we were told, of course, Mandeville would have had Forcier tell that one, because Forcier was the best there was. It seems apparent to me that Mandeville had a quite definite plan for the book, chose his stories carefully, and deferred to the best storyteller for that one very crucial story.

ON THE STRUCTURE OF THE FULL SET

In *Chipewyan Texts* (Li & Scollon 1976) we published, in plain prose form, all of the stories except two, "His Grandmother Raised Him" and "How I Made a Canoe" (stories 4 and 19). We omitted the latter simply because it had recently been published on its own (as Li 1964).

As I have mentioned, people at Fort Chipewyan thought the collection was incomplete without "His Grandmother Raised Him." But another set of stories, which we did include, also caused some puzzlement. These were the stories that form Part Two: Elicited Accounts (stories 17–21). At Fort Chipewyan people responded to these texts rather differently than to the main body of the stories. With these they would merely comment that, yes, François was an adept builder of everything from canoes and boats to houses. When saying this, they would often point to his house, still standing there some fifty years after it was built.

When I discussed this with Professor Li, he pointed out to me that these stories dealt with topics he had asked Mandeville to talk about. They were not spontaneously chosen by Mandeville and were not part of his own selection of narratives. In this book I have rearranged the stories to reflect this. All of the stories in Part One were chosen by Mandeville, and they are printed here in the sequence he chose. Part Two consists of the five accounts dictated at Li's suggestion. The first two of these were told as they began the work; the latter three came as later interruptions to Mandeville's program.

Finally, a word on the termination of Mandeville's selection. My notes covering my discussions with Professor Li on that summer's work tell me that Li believed that Mandeville had exhausted his repertoire when he finished the two Wise Man stories (stories 15 and 16). From Li's point of view, he was ready to stop because he didn't know any more stories. Philip Mandeville gives a different but convincing account. He told me that his father knew many, many more stories but that his father had told the best ones. Perhaps it is also important to know that Philip said that the two Wise Man stories were his father's favorite stories. He had saved the best for last.

In a strict sense I would only want to claim that the stories of Part

One constitute what I have called the narrative ethnography. Nevertheless there is much of interest in the other five stories.

THE TEXT AND FORMATS OF THE SEQUENCE OF VERSIONS

Li's original transcriptions run along from line to line and make no use of punctuation, spacing, or any other scribal means of indicating the story structure. He does indicate word breaks in most cases. This is probably because Mandeville separated words or word groups in dictating the stories. In other words, spaces in the original ten notebooks most likely indicate short pauses taken by Mandeville. Li was very careful not to introduce any further lexical or grammatical analysis as he took down the dictations. Of course, when he and Mandeville went back over the stories, Li was able to confirm his notions about the boundaries around lexical units by what Mandeville would accept as a bona fide lexical item.

Chipewyan Texts (Li & Scollon 1976) was published with punctuation for sentences based on our analysis of sentence structure for Athabaskan, which by then was quite well developed for other languages as well. The next level of discourse structuring, however, was nearly completely arbitrary. In this we followed Li's 1964 publication (the first published version of "How I Made a Canoe") by making paragraph breaks just wherever it seemed to be about right from our intuitions about story content. Our purpose was simply to make it convenient for a linguist to cross-reference the Chipewyan and English facing translation pages. (The appendix to this book includes a four-page example.)

What I wanted to do here is to highlight the readability of Mandeville's narrative ethnography. The focus is on the content, not the structure of the stories. As such, it is not strictly designed as a contribution to ethnopoetics. Still the book would not exist without the important work in ethnopoetics of Dell Hymes, Virginia Hymes, Dennis Tedlock, Barre Toelken, Richard and Nora Dauenhauer, Regna Darnell, and, before them, as their inspiration, Melville Jacobs. (A number of important works by these authors are listed in the bibliography, page 285.)

When I was working with Li on the 1976 book, I was just becoming aware of the central idea that oral narratives such as Mandeville's were as fully and carefully structured as major works in Western literary history. Following Hymes and the other authors mentioned, I have developed the presentation of the texts in this book based on explicit markers of discourse structure, which Mandeville used to show the internal logic of the narrative. I have published the analyses underlying the translation in several articles (Scollon 1976, 1977, 1979a, 1979b) and, together with Suzanne Scollon, in two books (Scollon & Scollon 1979, 1981) on Chipewyan and Athabaskan narrative.

STRUCTURAL MEANINGS

I will make a few explanatory comments here concerning what each of these levels of structure entails about narrative meanings.

(1) *Lines*

In this translation I have been somewhat less concerned with line turnings than others working in ethnopoetics. On the whole it has worked out that each line consists of a clause. Naturally problems arise in several cases. Where vocatives are used ('Grandson,' 'Grandmother'), I have continued the speech of the character on the following line. Where clause subordination occurs, I have in some cases chosen to invert the clauses in the English translation for greater readability. For example, in "The Cannibal" (story 8), there are the lines,

> *Even though he tried to force his way ahead,*
> *something kept pulling him back.*

This could have been more faithfully translated as,

> *Something kept pulling him back,*
> *even though he tried to force his way ahead.*

The inversion seems to me a minor breach of fidelity to the original, and I have allowed overall readability to determine the sequence.

(2) *Quotations*

There are two kinds of quotations in Mandeville's stories: those in which the narrator reports the exact speech of one of the characters, and embedded quotations in which a character quotes another character. In the Chipewyan these are clearly marked in almost every case with a verb of saying ('he said,' 'she told him,' 'they said to each other') both before and after the quoted speech. I have used a somewhat more elaborate set of verbs in English than is present in Chipewyan. For example, I have sometimes used 'answered' where the original has only 'said.' Chipewyan has a somewhat narrower range of such verbs of saying than English, and where the meaning was clear I have introduced some variety in the English.

In oral storytelling there are, of course, no punctuation marks, but verbs of saying routinely follow as well as precede the reported speech. In most cases I have let the closing punctuation marks (") and (') stand in for the redundant closing verb of saying.

Both types of reported speech are treated the same in that I have placed a half-line space both before and after the quotation. It should be noted that in some cases the following line may also begin a new verse (that is, a new sub-episode), but I have not, in such cases, doubled the spacing. There is a half-line space after any quotation, regardless of whether or not the quotation concludes what I call a verse.

(3) *Verses*

Verses are about the level of prose paragraphs in written discourse. Having said that, I should also say that they vary considerably in length from single-line verses to verses of as many as ten lines. They are rarely longer than that. The most common markers of a verse are the Chipewyan words *kúú* ('then'), and *'ɛkwą́t'uú* ('thus'). They mark well over half the verses in the corpus. But others with meanings such as 'suddenly,' 'quickly,' 'finally,' and 'therefore' are not at all uncommon. Generally speaking, a verse is the smallest unit of action (or explanation). It is a shift in the action focus which is keyed by these markers.

(4) *Stanzas*

Verses group together to constitute stanzas. The most common marker of the stanza by far is the word *'ɛkúú* ('then'). The reader will notice the similarity of the verse marker (*kúú*) and the stanza marker (*'ɛkúú*). Elsewhere (Scollon 1977) I have argued that the shorter form is, in fact, a phonological reduction. For other speakers this form can be further reduced to *húú, hú,* or even *ú*. We do not know whether this clear distinction of verse and stanza marking is unique to François Mandeville. He is certainly the most careful narrator in this aspect of discourse marking that we have on record. We also know that in the notebooks he sometimes corrected this form either 'up' or 'down' structural levels.

But *'ɛkúú* is not the only marker of stanza levels of discourse. Other markers include any words which indicate a major shift in time or place. The following three sentences excerpted from "The Wise Man – Story One" (story 15) mark the beginnings of stanzas:

> *For a long time the wise man didn't speak ...*
>
> *So that's how they came to the place with the open water ...*
>
> *After the shelters were all built, he said,...*

In a few words, the stanza is the level of discourse structure in which a sequence of actions or activities (or explanations) are logically grouped, often by action within a timespan. It is the logic of the grouping more than the specific linguistic markers which give cohesion to the stanza.

(5) *Scenes*

Hymes (1976) has remarked that in the hierarchy of levels of discourse, it is the scene which is the most difficult to establish analytically. This is certainly so in Chipewyan, because there are rarely specific linguistic markers for this level of structure, or to put it another way, the one marker we do have is *'ɛkúú*, which is already doing a major discursive task in marking the boundaries of verses. In these stories by far the most frequent basis I have found for marking a change in scene is the combination of the verse marker *'ɛkúú* together with a change in season or a major passage of time. Through the process of translating I have noticed that the shift of scene most frequently begins with a scene-final foreshadowing of the following scene, which is then clearly marked as a new scene. For example, in "The Man Who Hibernated with a Bear" (story 9), the change from Scene II to Scene III is as follows:

[SCENE II]

Then at last when the berries had ripened,

    the bear said,

        "Let's stay here where there are berries.
        The rapids aren't far away.
        We have arrived.

        "When we're done here at the berries
        we'll live by the fish in the rapids."

So they stayed there at the berries.

[SCENE III]

Finally autumn came.

In some cases the shift in scenes is between narrative action and narrative explanation, evaluation, or assessment. In "How Copper Was Discovered" (story 1), Act I, Scene II consists of an explanation of the practices of the 'barren-land enemy' (the Inuit) when they have captured someone in war and brought that person back to their home. At that point the scene shifts from a general explanation of practices back into the action as follows:

[ACT I, SCENE III]

That was their custom and so they now brought the woman in.

(6) *Acts*

Most of the stories amount to one-act stories. In those cases (ten of the sixteen) only scenes have been indicated in the translation. In six of them, however, there is a great enough break in the story continuity to amount to a new act. "How Copper Was Discovered" (story 1), for example, consists of five separate acts. The first act deals with the war between the Chipewyans and the Inuit and the consequent capture of the woman who ultimately makes the discovery of the metal. The first act ends when the chief decides that she should not be killed but should be married into his family as a slave. The opening of the next act finds the woman carrying a baby who can already speak a little as she tries to make her escape and return to her own people.

(7) *Parts*

One story, "Raven Head" (story 3), was separated in the original notebooks with spaces which indicated that the parts were dictated separately. Each of the four parts is given a separate initial (see initials below) but no separate title. This seemed justification for considering these to be four parts of a single story rather than separate stories as I did in the cases of Old Axe (stories 6 and 7) and the Wise Man (stories 15 and 16).

(8) *Prologues and Initials*

As Jacobs (1959) noted for his materials, virtually all of the stories begin with an initial. This is a 'once upon a time' sentence. Here, for example, are the openings of Mandeville's first five stories:

> *Long ago the people fought the barren-land enemy …*
>
> *There was a man named Beaver Orphan …*
>
> *In the summer many people were camped together …*
>
> *Once, people were camped …*
>
> *There was a boy whose body was covered with scabs …*

The initial sets the frame for the story to follow. This frame most often is simply that people were camped or staying in a place. This initial is often, but not always, followed by the word *sni*. The most common translation is the one I have used here, 'This is what they say.' The form itself is peculiar as it is based on the verb stem '*–ni*' ('to say') but has the verb prefix '*s-*' which is not found as the lone prefix to a verb stem anywhere else. The form *sni* may possibly be a reduction of the so-called fourth-person pronominal verb prefix plus the stem 'to say': *tsʼɛ + ni*, 'someone says.'

In many cases, but not all, the initial is extended into a prologue which sets the stage for the story in more detail. The prologue for "His Grandmother Raised Him" (story 4) is characteristic:

> *Once, people were camped.*
>
> *An old woman who was raising her grandson*
> *stayed there along with the other people.*

(9) Epilogues and Finals

The closing frame of the story is much like the opening frame but in reverse. There is often, but not always, an epilogue in which conclusions are drawn or the story is in some way tied up and finished. Often there is simply a final which in some cases is just the last line of the last scene.

The epilogue and final from the second Wise Man story (story 16) are characteristic:

> *So that's how they all slid downward to the lake, one after the other.*
>
> *He clubbed down all the enemy band*
> *even though he was alone by himself.*
> *This is what they say.*

The second line of this excerpt is broken, and the second line indented, only for typographic convenience.

Note that the final most often ends with the Chipewyan form *sni*, 'This is what they say.'

The epilogue to "The Cannibal" (story 8) is quite heavily salted with this marker *sni,* and it is only in this epilogue that the relation between the cannibal and the mosquito is clearly explained:

[EPILOGUE]

When the leaves change color in the fall
they disappear instantly.
This is what they say.

These are mosquitoes.
This is what they say.

The Cannibal was stupid,
and the mosquitoes were his brain.
This is what they say.

The mosquitoes were part of the Cannibal.
That's why mosquitoes like to eat people's blood.
This is what they say.

The story structure throughout these stories, then, is remarkably well indicated by Mandeville to consist of a hierarchy of elements, represented in my translation as follows:

Title

[MAIN DIVISION (ACT, SCENE, ETC)]

Stanza (*flush with left margin; half a line space following*)

    Verse (*one indent; half a line space following*)
    Line (*takes preceding level of indent; no line spaces between lines*)

        "Narrator quoted speech or thoughts"
        (*double indents; double quotation marks*)

            'Character quoted speech or thoughts'
            (*triple indents; single quotation marks*)

In the following short excerpt from "Raven Head" (story 3), we can see an illustration of these levels of meaning for an internal segment of the story:

[ACT I, SCENE I]

Raven Head's younger sister made a birchbark cup for him.
    (Stanza, flush left)

He had it tied on, (Verse, one indent)
but whenever they drank water, he said, (Line)

   "Lend me a cup so I can drink."
      (Narrator quotation, double indent)

He said this every time. (Verse, one indent)

Finally one of them wondered, (Verse, one indent)

   "Why does he say that? (Narrator quotation, double indent)
   He has a cup, (Line)
   but whenever we drink water, he says, (Line)

      'Lend me a cup.'" (Character quotation, triple indent)

Raven Head answered him, (Stanza, flush left)

   "I can't drink from my cup. (Narrator quotation, double indent)
   My sister's making fun of me." (Line)

He didn't say anything else. (Stanza, flush left)

(10) *How This Works in Practice*

The structural outlining that is presented in these stories and the placement on the page is quite consistent within and throughout this set of stories. This was done with an interactive process as follows.

First of all I selected the four stories on which I had developed my earlier analyses (Scollon 1976, 1977, 1979a, 1979b). From these I was able to extract the several very clear and formal linguistic markers of textual divisions ('ɛkúú, kúú, 'ɛkwą́t'uú, and the rest). For each story, then, I marked up the Chipewyan text for initials and finals, prologues and epilogues, acts where these seemed to be justified, scenes, stanzas, verses, quotations, and lines. This gave a provisional structure.

Then I marked the text for the secondary or less frequent markers of structure. In very few cases did this call the previous marking into question.

Next I began to make a translation into English guided by this discourse structure and based on Li's original interlinear word translations, the translation in the 1976 book, and my own retranslation from the original Chipewyan.

This process both resolved earlier questions and then raised the possibility of new markers. Where content, the narrative action sequencing, the participants in the narrative, and the syntax agreed that there was a discursive break in the text, that provided new candidates for new markers. Those new candidates were then tested in three ways. First they were tested against the sense and flow of the original story in Chipewyan. Clearly, as I went along and became refamiliarized with the language, my ability to simply read the originals improved rapidly. Second, these new candidates were tested against possible English translations. Finally I reviewed all of the previously translated stories to see if introducing these new markers would seriously disrupt the existing structure and translation.

I found there were almost no cases where going back in this way really distorted or seriously altered the earlier structuring and translation. On the contrary, in almost every case this new candidate proved to make the text and its translation more intelligible.

In an early paper (Scollon 1977) I showed that taking such discourse structuring seriously could point to aspects of the narrative which were not otherwise overtly marked. There is a point in the construction of a canoe at which the formerly loose pieces of bark and framing become a tight whole. This canoe is then turned over so that the outer side can be worked on. There is no mention in Mandeville's narrative of the action of turning the canoe over and repositioning it for the subsequent action. This change in perspective is only indicated through the use of a discourse marker.

Likewise I found as I learned new ways in which verses, stanzas, scenes, and acts could be marked, these proved to open up insights into the structure of the texts I had translated before I was aware of this structuring. This iterative method did not actually add very many new words, phrases, or other linguistic markers to the original inventory, but it did produce a progressively improving sense of clarity to both the original narrative and the consequent translation.

ACTION MARKING THROUGH ASPECT AND TENSE

Translating from Chipewyan into English requires attention to the grammatical distinction between aspect and tense. Most languages express both aspect and tense, but most are based on one or the other system of marking time. Chipewyan, like all of the other Athabaskan languages, is based on aspect. English, like all of the other Indo-European languages, is based on tense. After a few words about the differences between aspect and tense, I will comment on a few areas where this is important in understanding these narratives. Unfortunately, like all translators, I will have to ask the reader to return to the original Chipewyan narratives for a fuller understanding of Mandeville's use of aspect in telling these stories.

Chipewyan verbs are marked for aspect, not for tense. Tense marking is done through independent particles, and this is somewhat rare. While the grammatical structures of both aspect and tense tell us something about time, aspect focuses on the nature and duration of the actions of verbs, and tense focuses on the sequencing of actions on a time line from past through the present and into the future. In Chipewyan the main aspects are imperfective, perfective of which there are two forms, optative, iterative, and progressive. The action in an imperfective verb is one which is unbounded in time, or unmarked for time. The verb does not tell us when an action begins nor when it ends, only that it exists. Perhaps the closest English translation is the present tense verb in a sentence like, 'I tell a story.' This is something which I do but the sentence does not say whether I am telling the story right now, have told it in the past, or will tell it in the future. This imperfective aspect is the unmarked aspect in Chipewyan. That is, it has no verb prefixes to indicate the imperfective aspect. Imperfective aspect is marked by the verb stem alone.

The action in a perfective verb is one which is clearly bounded. It has a beginning and an end, but unlike a tense system, this action may take place at any time from in the past through the present or in the future. In Chipewyan it would be something like 'story told.' It would cover all of the sentences in English from 'I told a story,' 'I had told a story,' 'I have told a story,' to 'I will have told a story.' The Chipewyan perfective does not say anything about when this action was performed, just that it was a clearly bounded action.

Chipewyan has two perfective prefixes which add a distinction to the perfective marking of the verb stem. One of them, $\gamma\varepsilon$, indicates that the action was completed in the past but that it no longer is the case. If I say, 'They lay down' (as in "The Man Who Became a Wolf," story 11) with the $\gamma\varepsilon$ perfective prefix, I am saying that in the next action they are no longer lying down. If I say, 'They lay down' with the $\theta\varepsilon$ perfective prefix, I am implying that the next action I narrate occurs while they are still lying down. To translate this into English for the first case I would need to say, 'They lay down. Then after getting up she said....' To translate the second I would need to say 'They lay down. Some time after that she said ...,' which would leave the question of their getting up unaddressed but would capture the durative force of the $\theta\varepsilon$ perfective. In this translation I have chosen in most cases not to insert these epenthetic clarifications where it seemed they were not necessary. In this quotation from story 11, for example, I have thought it clear enough that the old wolf was now awake after a long sleep because she was speaking to the man who had become a wolf. But in the Chipewyan original there is a clear marking through the use of aspect of this 'silent' action of getting up from sleep.

The optative aspect is easily confused with the future tense as the action is one which has not yet occurred but which the speaker anticipates occurring. The key is the hypothetical nature of the optative. It is an action which is neither bounded nor unbounded, as it does not yet exist. In this way the optative is sometimes considered to belong to the modal system rather than the aspect system. It is not much used in these narratives, though there is a good example of these aspects playing together at the start of the first scene of story 11. The old wolf tells Spread Wings,

> *"If you want* [imperfective]
>   *to live longer* [optative] *on the earth*
> *you must live* [imperfective] *with us again.*
> *If you do that* [perfective]
>   *you will live* [imperfective] *for a long time."*

The 'wanting' is construed as unbounded. It is not a momentary or narrow impulse, but something Spread Wings would feel at any time. 'To live longer' is set as an anticipated action by the optative. 'You must live with us' is construed as unbounded but then reconstrued as finished by the perfective in the next sentence. Finally, the result would be imperfective – living for a long unbounded time.

Progressive and iterative aspects are also not much used. The progressive is much like progressive in English except that no time is marked. 'I am writing,' 'I was writing,' and 'I will be writing' would be simply 'writing (is going on at the moment I am narrating).' The customary aspect indicates that the action is repetitive either in a short time span or in the sense that the action is something that someone does regularly or even normatively. I will give an example of customary below.

There are three kinds of narratives in this collection of stories. The largest group could be called mythological (stories 1 to 16). These are followed by two stories that might be called procedural in that they relate what is normally or commonly done but do not include either mythological figures nor are they explicitly taken from the life of the narrator (stories 17 and 18). The final three are narratives of Mandeville's own personal experience (stories 19 to 21).

Aspect relates directly to this overall typology of narratives. The narratives of mythological time (stories 1 to 16) are predominantly a sequence of actions in the perfective. There are exceptions, of course, such as when complex actions are embedded within each other. The same is true for narratives of personal experience (stories 19 to 21).

The sequence of actions in the perfective often corresponds to a sequence of actions in real time in the past. Note that this is an assumed correspondence. We have no independent evidence of how Mandeville made a canoe, tanned a moose hide, or hunted beavers. Also in the mythological stories the 'real time' is not, in fact, the same cosmological time as that in which Mandeville made a canoe. But more importantly, the narrated sequence does not indicate other than through the narrating in real time what the real time sequence of actions was. An example of this divergence from a time-line tense sequential order occurs in story 19:

> *When that was done* [perfective],
> *the woman sewed the sides for me* [perfective].
> *I put the gunwale on* [perfective]
> *and also trimmed the sides* [perfective] *above the gunwale.*
> *The woman sewed the bow posts* [perfective] *down for me.*
> *Then I put the inside keel* [perfective] *in the canoe.*
>
> *I put the small endpieces* [perfective] *on the keel*
> *and made the props* [perfective] *for the bow posts.*
>
> *I had made the keel* [perfective] *much too long,*
> *so I cut a part of it off* [perfective] *to the correct length.*

Notice in the last line of the first verse quoted here, he put the keel into the canoe. This is in the perfective. In the first line of the third verse he repeats this action with the qualification that it was too long and needed to be cut. The English past perfect 'I had made the keel too long' covers this fairly well, but it is important to see that there is nothing in the Chipewyan to indicate that this action is out of sequence. Put another way, there is nothing in the Chipewyan which sequences any of the actions given here. The perfective only conveys that each action was a separate action. If I may put this yet another way, narrative sequencing is not done grammatically here but through the oral sequencing in the telling as well now as with the placement on the page.

Another more important example of how an aspect system may layer multiple time perspectives on a sequence of actions occurs just after this section of the same story:

> *Then I spread* [imperfective] *hot water all over it.*
>
> *That heated* [perfective] *the birchbark throughout.*
> *I carefully tapped* [progressive] *the ribs into place,*
> *one after another* [iterative].

In that way I adjusted them [perfective]
finally into their proper place.

That made the birchbark stretch quite tight [perfective]
on the frame of the canoe.

We do not know exactly how he spread the hot water but we can assume that in order to thoroughly soak the birchbark by heating water in a kettle over a campfire, it took quite some time. More importantly, he would have had to finish the task of adjusting the ribs while the canoe was still wet. So however he did the wetting, it was an action which went on across the whole time period taken up by the subsequent actions. Setting this in the imperfective opens up the boundary of the wetting event to encompass the following actions.

As to those actions, he puts the tapping of the ribs into the progressive aspect, which indicates that this is what he was doing while the imperfective aspect of the wetting remained open. He then shifts to the iterative to convey that this action was repeated again and again multiple times for each of the many canoe ribs. He finally closes the time frame by grouping the whole sequence of actions ('in that way') and employing the perfective ('I adjusted them'). The deictic pronoun 'that' refers anaphorically back to the sequence beginning from soaking the birchbark to the completion with the dry stretched bark.

A word needs to be said about the procedural narratives in stories 17 and 18. These are set apart from the other two groups of narratives by the predominant use of the imperfective throughout. This has posed the most general problem for translation. I have used what we might call the anthropological past to translate these two stories but, I must confess, it does not fit very well with the original use of the imperfective. We can look at one example as I have translated it and then compare that with what might have been done had I wanted to hew the aspect line more closely. In story 17 there is the section that follows:

When an old man called for all the children,
they all came to him.

Then he told the children about a long time in the past,
about all of those who could do things well,

those who had strong powers,
those who were fast,
or those who could hunt well and how they did that.

He told the children stories about those capable people
and about what they did that made them unlike others.

An alternative which would try to capture the imperfective setting of the original might be as follows:

When an old man calls for all the children,
they all come to him.

Then he tells the children about a long time in the past,
about all of those who can do things well,
those who have strong powers,
those who are fast,
or those who can hunt well and how they do that.

He tells the children stories about those capable people
and about what they do that makes them unlike others.

For two reasons I have rendered these stories in the anthropological past, however. The first is that in English the persistent use of the present sounds to my ears a bit jokey or informal. The second is that throughout these narratives, Mandeville interlaces phrases such as 'in the past,' or 'a long time ago,' which suggest to me a need to be clear that he was talking about how things might be in a somewhat idealized situation which, in practice, he might have seen as lying largely in the past even in 1928 when he told the stories.

There are a few specialized uses of aspect in the stories which are also interesting. The most common opening of the myth narratives is either an introduction of the main character by name or with a statement that people were camped together as noted above. The initial to story 2, for example is,

There was a man named Beaver Orphan.

The verb 'named' is given in the imperfective. In this case the name is taken to be an unbounded state. He is always named Beaver Orphan. This is not because this could not be said in the perfective. In Li's notes there are such examples. When the perfective is used it conveys the idea that the naming is concluded; the person is no longer named that. All of the initials in these narratives which give names, give them with imperfective verbs.

This is a more general phenomenon, however. The most common other initial is to say that people were camped together. The verb 'to be staying' is also always given in the imperfective. Again, this could be otherwise. In the initial of Mandeville's story of his own beaver hunting, he says,

> One winter we camped near beavers.

This initial is given in the perfective, the $\gamma\varepsilon$ perfective which conveys the idea that this camping was finished back then and not repeated. That is, it was not a regular place where they camped.

The idea of regular or continued camping is found at the end of story 17, where we see the following:

> Again, after they ate,
>   they would make packs of meat
>   and pack off all the meat.
>
> Nearly all the days would pass, one by one, in this way,
>   as they stayed with him.

Both the actions of packing and carrying meat back to camp and the camping itself are given the iterative aspect for events that happen iteratively.

In other words, initials in the sixteen stories all are set in the imperfective. They are not given boundaries in time. They are told without reference to time in the real world of the narrator's time. One further point is that when it is said that 'people' are camping, this verb is given the so-called fourth-person prefix ts'ε. While this prefix is rare in normal use, it is common for initials of myth stories. This pronoun indicates an indefinite 'somebody.' It is something like the use of 'one' in English

('One was camped') except that it does not suggest that the 'one' is the narrator nor even that it is singular. It is simply an indefinite person or persons.

These points about initials are true as well of the two procedural stories but not of the narratives of personal experience. In those three stories Mandeville sets the actions definitely as bounded events by using the perfective as I have just noted for his beaver hunt (story 21).

Finally, in the originals of these stories, verbs of saying are given in the imperfective. To return to the opening of story 11, which I quoted above, if I had wanted to render these verbs more closely in English I might have written,

> When he is very old, a wolf speaks to him,
>
>> "If you want to live longer on the earth,
>> you must live with us again.
>> If you do that,
>> you will live for a long time."
>
> Spread Wings thinks,
>
>> "I don't want to be a wolf again."
>
> But the wolf says,
>
>> "If you do not become a wolf again,
>> you will die soon."
>
> Spread Wings answers,
>
>> "I want to live longer on the earth,
>> so I will become a wolf again."

To my ear this is awkward and sounds inappropriate for this kind of narrative. I have therefore used the past tense forms 'spoke,' 'thought,' 'said,' and 'answered.' I admit, however, that in doing so we lose the sense of perennial and unbounded action which is felt when the stories are heard or read in Chipewyan.

MANDEVILLE'S NARRATIVE ETHNOGRAPHY
IN THE CHIPEWYAN ORAL NARRATIVE TRADITION

As I have said, my organizing goal was to produce a readable translation that would at once be answerable to the original texts in Chipewyan and in which the reader could have a high degree of confidence that the translator would not be playing free and loose with the discourse structure. The general methodology I have used seems to me as valid for these stories as we are likely now to ever get. We cannot go back now and interview Mandeville or ask him to tell us new stories. We cannot go back and ask Professor Li what his intentions were or if he had clues about narrative structure which he hadn't already put either into his notes or his comments to me as we worked on the 1976 book.

But to what extent can we generalize from this set of stories to 'Chipewyan narrative'? This is, of course, a much more difficult question having to do with the ways in which the language is sociolinguistically distributed across the geography of northern Canada, with the ways in which the language has undergone historical and sociolinguistic change in the eighty years since 1928, and the contexts in which the stories were told.

I have in my files the preparations for another set of analyses and translations which might shed light on this question. I have collected nine versions of the story "His Grandmother Raised Him" (story 4 in this book). These were recorded by the Oblate priest Émile Petitot circa 1863 (four versions), the anthropologist Robert Henry Lowie in 1912 (one version), the anthropologist Pliny Earle Goddard in 1913 (one version), by Li Fang-kuei in 1928 (one version), and by myself in 1977 (two versions). My still-preliminary analysis shows that these stories are structured around a common skeleton story. That is, while the stories vary widely in length and in the details which are narrated, an analysis by line, verse, stanza, scene, and act such as I have used in the stories in this book shows surprising consistency in the core framework of the story even across more than a century (1863 to 1977), among different storytellers, and in a variety of places where Chipewyan is spoken. Of all of the versions, Forcier's is the most succinct.

This raises a host of questions, only some of which I can address here. Central among the questions is this: Why is this story as Forcier tells it so parsimonious, especially given the fact that he was considered by both Mandeville in 1928 and by people at Fort Chipewyan in 1977 to be one of the best of storytellers? Wouldn't that lead us to expect a more fully elaborated and detailed story?

There are at least four factors which may contribute to Forcier's succinctness: the place in modern history of the narration, the religious or secular identity of the audience for the story, Forcier's comfort with the situation of the dictation, and the degree to which the audience seemed, to the storyteller, knowledgeable in the storytelling tradition. Some of this is discussed at greater length elsewhere (Scollon & Scollon 1979, 1981, 1984).

My all too sketchy survey of multiple versions of these stories suggests that there have been two influences on the Chipewyan narrative tradition in the past hundred years. The first of these is the development of liturgical materials, mostly in the syllabic script used throughout this part of North America (see Bringhurst 2008). Liturgical materials written in Chipewyan syllabics show quite definite uses of discourse marking forms (especially the forms 'ɛkúú and kúú). I feel certain that further study would give good evidence that this usage reflects 'chapter and verse' structuring imitated from Chipewyan translations of the Bible. When Petitot recorded his stories in 1863, it is unlikely that either he or his narrators would have had significant exposure to Chipewyan syllabic writing. The script was in local use from about 1852 and the first publication was in 1857 in Montreal (Bringhurst 2008: 19). Thus the narrators were quite unlikely to have been influenced by this careful paragraphing. Conversely, Mandeville was an avid reader of church materials, and Ben Marcel, with whom I worked in 1976–77, was a lay reader in the church. We cannot rule out that Chipewyan ethnopoetic structuring in the period of the twentieth century was strongly influenced by liturgical materials such as the translation of the Bible into Chipewyan syllabics. In fact, at Fort Chipewyan in 1977, Victoria Mercredi insisted that we learn syllabics, which we did. She felt that otherwise we could not understand the Chipewyan language.

The second influence on Chipewyan narrative tradition is simply the rapid increase in communication and transportation during the twentieth century. Mandeville himself was an excellent example of a person who ranged throughout almost the entire length and breadth of Chipewyan territory in the course of a lifetime of work as the Hudson's Bay Company and other traders extended their networks of commerce. His contacts both across sub-dialects of Chipewyan and with neighboring languages gave him a kind of historical-comparative sensibility to language contrasts which afforded him a quite normative and conservative sense of the Chipewyan language – not unlike the sense of language normally achieved by formally trained linguists (Scollon & Scollon 1979).

Over time, ways of using the language that were first introduced through writing came to seem natural, or even traditional, to native speakers. Also, as more people had the experience of hearing how people in other places spoke their language and also the related neighboring languages, they began to take on more fixed pronunciations. It is not surprising to me that Mandeville as well as Forcier – and then, closer to the present, Ben Marcel – used a language that reflected these historical changes.

But one should be careful about imagining that the stories Petitot recorded were more authentically Chipewyan because they were recorded earlier in time and therefore less influenced by these modernizing conditions of communication and literacy. When he tells the story "His Grandmother Raised Him," he launches directly into the main character's anger with the people and his wish to leave their camp. Two kinds of content are used in many of the other versions to prepare the listener for this anger.

First, in most of the versions there is a somewhat extended presentation of the scene in which the lead character (HGRH, let us call him) is discovered. He is tiny: so small that he has hidden under a pile of caribou excrement. He is found either by a young girl or an old woman, and she finds him because he is crying. In gratitude, he takes good care of his rescuer and her people by always providing them with caribou tongues to eat. Thus we know of his character and the indebtedness of the woman and the people to him. That is found in some form in almost all of the stories. In fact, in the version told to me by Fred Marcel (Ben Marcel's younger brother), this is all that is revealed:

A boy was found in the moss by his grandmother. After he grew up some he told his grandmother how to do things and they lived good. He killed caribou by biting the end of their tongues.

But the second type of material in the prologue section occurs only in the stories told to the Oblate priest Petitot. There HGRH begins by enjoining the people to treat him well. In essence he exacts tribute from them in exchange for his caring for them. Unfortunately, the people begin to slip in their appreciation of HGRH, and so he embarks on a path of anger and retribution. It is impossible for my ears not to hear fierce Old Testament stories of divine retribution resonating in the background in these stories told to a priest. As in Mandeville's conclusion to "The Adventures of Beaulieu" (story 10) in which Beaulieu sees the error of his ways, converts to the priest's religion, and spends the rest of his life in acts of penance, it is difficult to imagine these themes outside of the religious teachings of the priests who were such a great influence across the world of the Chipewyans.

There is yet a more important reason to question the authenticity of the narratives recorded by Petitot and some others of that period to which Bringhurst (2004, 2006) has called attention. Petitot and others were concerned with learning Chipewyan for the purpose of bringing European culture, mostly liturgical materials, to the Chipewyan people. Their interest was not like that of Boas, Sapir, or Li to record what the storyteller said as authentically and accurately as possible. There is good reason to think that Petitot thought that the Chipewyan stories needed to be improved by adding elements of judgment, retribution, and narrative force, or by altering the sequencing and presentation of details. We cannot now go back and do further research on the circumstances in which Petitot did his work, but I agree with Bringhurst that in the stories recorded by Petitot, we are probably seeing more of Petitot than we are of his narrators.

A third factor that might have led to Forcier's brevity in telling "His Grandmother Raised Him" would be his lack of comfort with the situation he was in. Although he might have been good as a storyteller, he surely had little or no experience of telling stories for the purposes of dictation. Li told me very clearly that Mandeville was among the best of the people he worked with in any language at giving clear and careful dictations. Forcier would not have had Mandeville's experience of translating and dictating in public.

Furthermore, Forcier might also have been uncomfortable with the presence of a person from outside of the community. It is well known in linguistic and ethnopoetic work that those who are considered by the community to be the most central figures are difficult to approach from outside and are often relatively little experienced in dealing directly with outsiders. A common way of expressing this discomfort is to say as little as possible.

Finally, there is yet a fourth factor to consider in seeking to account for the brevity of Forcier's version of HGRH and that is the narrator's assessment of the knowledge of his or her audience. In other analyses we have done of Athabaskan storytelling (Scollon & Scollon 1979, 1981, 1984) we have said that the way a story is told is by progressively unfolding it in interaction with the audience. We compared Ben Marcel's story about hunting beaver in both Chipewyan and English versions. We found that when he told the story in Chipewyan, he assumed rightly that I could not simply follow the story and so he told it without really taking the audience much into consideration. He simply dictated it. When he told the same story in English immediately afterward, I was following and supplying conventional audience responses. How he structured that version as well as the details he included were contingent on how I had responded to the verse or stanza he had just completed. Stories were expanded to the extent he felt necessary for my comprehension.

To summarize this, within the Athabaskan storytelling tradition one doesn't waste words or insult one's listener by telling somebody something he or she already knows. A truly knowledgeable person really only requires an allusion to the story. Simply to say the words 'His Grandmother Raised Him' conveys the cultural premises that we often are not able to judge the ability of others, that it is important to do this, and especially not to underestimate those who might appear to be small, weak, or deformed. Well-being of the individual and of the social group comes from paying close attention to and respecting the abilities of others. That's all Fred Marcel said when he 'told' the story, and Baptiste Forcier didn't say very much more.

Why, then, did Mandeville himself tell rather more extended versions of stories than Forcier did in this one instance? I think the crucial factor is that when Mandeville was speaking to Li, he knew him as a stranger to Chipewyan people and to the stories he was telling. Li needed details, and Mandeville gave them to him. When they went together to see Baptiste Forcier, however, Li was merely a scribe. I believe that Forcier told the story to Mandeville and showed his great skill by presenting the briefest précis extracted from all of the many versions and multiple details he would have known as the elder narrator that he was. It was the selection for Mandeville that makes this a good narration, not the paucity of detail.

In conclusion, it seems clear that Mandeville's narrative ethnography is quite an accomplished work. It steers an admirable course between profligate detailing for an ignorant audience and excessive brevity for an insider audience. It also steers a course between excessive influence of Christian liturgical texts and unrealistically conservative nativism. Finally, the stories are structured within a steadily developing and normalizing modern Chipewyan oral-literate tradition.

Appendix

Four States of an Oral Text

This appendix is adapted from *The Surface of Meaning: Books and Book Design in Canada* (Bringhurst 2008). It illustrates the progression of a short passage of text (the opening scenes of story 11, "The Man Who Became a Wolf") from Li Fang-kuei's 1928 field notebook through the prose form adopted in *Chipewyan Texts* (Li & Scollon 1976) to the form adopted for the present book, and back to a form that would have been familiar to Mandeville and might be used to return these texts at last to Chipewyan readers.

Pages 266–271 are digital facsimiles of pp 16–21 of Li's Chipewyan field notebook 8, reproduced with the kind permission of the American Philosophical Society Library, Philadelphia. (The story begins at the point marked by the marginal arrow, near the bottom of page 16 of the notebook.) Pages 272–275 are digital facsimiles of pp 322–325 of *Chipewyan Texts.* Pages 276–281 show the same text retranscribed and retranslated to reflect the inherent structure of Mandeville's original oral narrative (in essence the form employed throughout this book). Pages 282–284 are the same text, in the same arrangement, but in Chipewyan syllabics, the script in which François Mandeville himself was accustomed to read and write Chipewyan.

16

kǘʻ   sɔ̀ hò'èt,ìnčhʻɛ̀ ìˈl̩xà   daˈčdìːs 'aˊ
then   my sin s   in place of it   I'll make penance

t̩'aˈ hùˊk̩'ɛ̀ˊ   dɔ̀nɛ̀   t̩èɣaˊnɛ̀ɪ̀d̩d̩ɛ́nɛ̀
wherever   people   I had killed

dʒènɛˊ ɹu̯às·àˊ   daˈči̯odèːs 'àˊ hùˊkɛˊ
I'll go about   I'll make penance while

t̩ɔ̀n·ì   ˈìlsnaˊ 'àdʒaˊ hùˊ̩l̩dɔ̀ù̃   'àˈlàⁱ̀nɛ̀
he said   he has done that then   at one place

náɹ̩ì d̩ɔ̀n   d̩aˊ ɹìˈɔ̀ì naˊ   t̩ɛ̀ìˊ nèɪ̯
he had stayed long he has lived and his

k̩'ɛ̀nɛ̀   daˊnìt̩ɛ́aˊ   hùˊt̩dɔ̀ù̃
children   they are big   then

hùˊ ɹà̩   t̩èɣaˊnɛ̀ɪ̀ d̩·ɔ̀n
well   he died

dɔ̀nɛ̀   nɔ̀ùⁱmiˈy̆ɛ̀   ˈɛ̀nàˈd l̩ìˈ(ì)
person wolf   he (must.) becomes

t̩èɹà̩ hɔ̀n·ì
about him   the news; story

'įtáʔį̀ dǫ̀nè 'èdèʔìɬkàlʔ̀ híʔlʔyè
one   man   E.   he is called

'eyį̀ dǫ̀nè nǫ̀nìè hìnàdlíʔsnì
that man   wolf he becomes, they say
                     (cust.)

'eyį̀ nǫ̀nìè ʔìlíʔ łèáʔyà dǫ̀nè
that wolf he has become after man

hìnàddlį àʔ táʔlèlìnyè dàʔèʔtìʔ
he become again if   a young man he is like

'ànàtłį̀ snì tʔałt 'ètʔòyí hųłʔìdí
he becomes,does it's said 3 times well much
  (cust.)

nę̀ʔúʔnìłʔDʔrì hòtʔòʔn dǫ̀nè ʔìlíʔ
he is aged   till then a person he has been

snì ʔʔkùʔʔn 'į̀ʔtáʔ nǫ̀nèʔyè nàʔìdlíʔʔn
it is said then once   wolf he has been
                                      again

hòʔyà tòʔlnà 'ìkùʔʔn ʔìtʔòʔyí
about it he told at that time very

nę̀ʔúʔnìłʔDʔrì nàdlìʔʔn nǫ̀nìʔyè 'àyìʔt
he got old   again   a wolf told

nìʔ 'į̀ʔtìʔʔn níhòtìʔʔ nàʔwàsʔDʔrì
him yet   on the earth I'll stay

yìnį̀ dàn dé´ nùwàxét nų́nà nèddàn
you think if   with us   you stay again!

'èkàré `àné dgá´ dé yų̀ nàdé´ Òá´
If you did that if   in the future long time

oį̀ nà´ `ìnà y̓ètnì kí´ụ́ j̓àcìt k̓àlì`
you live will be he told him then   È.

nǫ̀ nìyè´ nàgwàs dlé´ k̓ìlè´ yènèdàn
wolf   I'll be again not   he thinks

k̓ìlè nǫ̀ nìyè `àg̓ètnì nǫ̀ nìyè
but   wolf   told him   wolf

k̓ènà` Oì`dlì` ìlì´ dé nèdìyè
you have become not if   you death
    again

ìnà Òá k̓ìlì´ y̓ètnì `àd èìt k̓àlì`
will be long not he told him   È.

`àdì `àtų́ụ́ nì` k̓ì k̓ì` ná gwàs Òàn
he said still on the earth   I'll stay

yìnìs Òàn `ėį̀ là´ nǫ̀ nìyè gwàsté´
I think on   therefore wolf   I'll be

k̓ènà` dèdàné nǫ̀ nìyè k̓ìÒìlì̀
he said above   wolf   he became

kúu 'iyá dághé nóniyé yétsòn
now   that   which wolf   to him

yátthòy ní   nóniyé   tséyá kúiyé
it was walking the wolf   an old woman

'iyá   'adè   híké   kúu 'id àt kálì
that it is speaking he found the   E.

nóniyé hèOílÈ   dàdàné   nóniyé
wolf   he has become at once   wolf

tséyá kúiyé   'aÿ'st ní súnàyè
woman   she said to him   my grandchild

yúutOé   'étO ní dà   lèsá   dó'è
to the north dear   many probably now

'èlawò zí   húi,tás héná 'èkúu
that way   we'll start she said then

yúutOé   hèóÿ 'à 'iyí nóniyè
to the north they started that   wolf

nú'ú níttòn kúlú ná'lttà'
she is old   but   she goes far

hítá' xúii nctèé kúlú hòð'aá
then   lake   big — even   it remains
= in no time —

hílé   yìhí'tdá nà l guí   'èkwí t'į
not   she goes (on all fours) to the   she does (again)
                            end of it (mist)

bįtá'ã   'ètsį'nàʋ   hò zų̀z hé'
while   finally   barren land on

nįhį́t'áz   'èkwí   'ètàxą 'ìttsùí
they came again   then   suddenly caribous

hó'jí   'àhųįjį'   bétšùné 'àyéłwí
tracks   they saw   his ? mother she told him

sįnàjį'   'èkwí   bóʋ bà hùʋdłsį
my son   now   we are hungry

dįwí   bèhó'jí   ʋílé 'įjí bóʋ
this   its track   we are looking that meat

'ą̀ t'į'   'èkwí sá   nį(hé nìtdòųłìtłí
it is   now ?   I got old   therefore

sà dįjí   kùlú   nòų teìlè lìųí
for me impossible   but   you   young man

nìlì   'įjí t'áʋ   nà dįjí hílé'
you are   therefore   for you impossible not

le'sá   nòų   bèhó'nìjí hègòàt
probably,   you   after it   you go!
I suppose

21

ʔɛ́kuːⁿ sɛ̀ nɛ̀hɛ́ nɛ̀gɛ̀ teu̇ sȧʔⁱ
then   I   after you   I'll start

ⁱt'axà ʔɛ́tθóⁿ tɛ̀gá nɛ̀ɬdòⁱ dɛ́
(suddenly / by chance) the caribous you have killed if

ⁱyɛ́ⁱ nɛ̀gù nɛ̀ nɛ̀oʒà ọmalɛ́ hɛ́nⁱ
there to you I came it will be he said

ʔɛ́kuːⁿ ʔⁱrù̇t hɛ̀lⁱ ʔɛ́tθóⁿ hɛ́nɛ̀gⁱ
then   F.   caribou after

tɛ̀ⁱdgà hòʒu̇ɛ́ hⁱⁱ nⁱ̀hⁱnⁱʔàznⁱ̀
he started barren grounds on they came

hu̇lⁱ ʔɛ̀d luⁱⁿ ʔⁱ̀t hⁱ́ⁱ dⁱtɛ̀ⁱⁿ yàgɛ̀
but   yet   some place   woods small

dárⁱ́dⁱà ⁱyⁱ́t'àⁱ ʔɛ́tθóⁿ hⁱt hⁱàt
they lie here + there those among caribous he is tracking

tɛ̀òⁱ ⁱⁱldgⁱnⁱ́ nⁱ̀d̀à ʔⁱ̀tθóⁿ nⁱ̀nⁱ̀t
night   moonlight   far   caribous he has

hⁱ́ hòʒu̇ɛ hⁱ́ hⁱ́ldgⁱⁿ tɛ̀ⁱ́ ⁱⁱt'àⁱ
tracked barren on   then   again in one place

àⁱtɛ̀ⁱⁿ yàgɛ̀ dⁱ́d̀ʔà̀ ʔⁱ́tθóⁿ nⁱ̀ògɛ̀
woods small   there is   caribou tracks

VIII.16-IX.10

12. The Story of the Man Who Became a Wolf

25)

1. There was a man called Spread Wings. It is
said that man became a wolf. It is said that when
he became a man again after being a wolf, he became
like a young man. Three times he lived until old
age and became a (young) man. So it is told about
how once again he became a wolf.

2. At that time, he having become very old
again, a wolf said to him, "If you wish to live on
the earth yet, you must live with us again . If you
do that, you will live for a long time in the future,"
it told him. Then Spread Wings thought, "I won't
be a wolf again." But the wolf told him, "If you
do not become a wolf again, it will not be long
until you die," he told him. Spread Wings said,
"I wish to live on the earth yet, so I'll become a
wolf," he said. At once he became a wolf.

12. dɛne nų̄niyɛ ʔɛnadlî· bɛyą̄ honi

1. ʔį̄ɫáyį̄ dɛne ʔɛdɛɫkali húlyɛ. ʔɛyi
dɛne nų̄niyɛ hɛnadlí sni. ʔɛyi nų̄niyɛ yį̄lé-tɫ'ą́yą̄
dɛne hɛnaθdlį̄-dé tcilekuyi láʔą̄t'ɛ ʔanat'į́ sni.
ta ʔoteyé hų́tɫ'éðé nį́únį̄θer hots'én dɛne
yį̄lé sni. ʔɛkú· ʔį̄ɫá nų̄niyɛ nayɛdlê· hoyą̄
holni.

2. ʔɛkú· ʔoteyé nį́únį̄θer nadlįú nų̄niyɛ
ʔayɛɫni. ʔą̄ɫų̆· nį̄ hok'ɛ náywasθer yɛnį̄ðen-dé
nuhwɛ-xéɫ nánanɛðer. ʔɛkwáʔanɛdjá-dé
yų·n̄aθé θá yį̄na-ixa, yéɫni. kú· ʔɛdɛɫkali,
nų̄niyɛ naywasdlé-híle yɛnį̄ðen. kúlú nų̄niyɛ
ʔayéɫni, nų̄niyɛ hɛnaθį̄dlį̄-híle-dé nɛðiyé-ixa
θá-híle, yéɫni. ʔɛdɛɫkali ʔadi, ʔą̄ɫų̆· nį̄
hok'ɛ náywasθer yɛnɛsθen ʔɛyit'á nų̄niyɛ ywasɫé,
héni. dɛdą̄né nų̄niyɛ hɛθɛlį̄.

VIII.16-IX.10

3. Then he found out that the wolf that was talking to him was an old woman. Then as soon as Spread Wings had become a wolf, the old woman said · to him, "My Grandson, there are probably many caribou to the North. Now we'll start out that way," she said. Then they started to the North.

4. That wolf was old, but since she went fast, she went to the end of the big lake in no time. And so doing they finally came again to the barren ground. Then suddenly they saw caribou tracks. His grandmother said to him, "My Grandson, we are hungry now. (This which left these) tracks which we are looking at is meat. Now since I am old it is impossible for me, but you are a young man. Therefore I suppose it is not impossible for you. You go after it. Then I'll start after you. If by chance you have killed the caribou, I will come to you," she said.

274

3.　kʊ́· ʔɛyi t'ahi nʊniyɛ yɛts'én yaɬtei-nį
nʊniyɛ ts'éyąkuyi ʔɛyi ʔadi-hik'é.　kʊ́·
ʔɛdɛɬkali nʊniyɛ hɛθɛlį dɛdąné nʊniyɛ ts'éyąkuyi
　　　　　　51)
ʔayéɬni,　sʊnayį,　yʊ·tθɛ́ ʔɛtθén ɬą-lɛsą́.
dʊhú ʔɛkozį́ hʊ̌·t'ás,　héni.　ʔɛkʊ́· yʊ·tθɛ́
hɛ̌·ð?az.

4.　ʔɛyi nʊniyɛ nį́únɨɬθer,　kʊ́lú náltɬa-hit'á
tu nɛtcá kʊ́lú hóð?ą-híle yɛk'é tθ'ánalguih.
ʔɛkwát'į-hįt'ʊ̌· ʔɛts'į́naθɛ́ hozué-k'ɛ nįhįt'az.
ʔɛkʊ́· ʔɛt'axą ʔɛtθén-kɛyé ʔahu·yɛ?į.　bɛtsʊné
ʔayéɬni,　sʊnayį,　ʔɛkʊ́· bér-ba hí·ðer.　diri
bɛkɛyé níl?į ʔɛyi bér ʔąt'ɛ.　ʔɛkʊ́· si
nį́únɨɬθer-hit'á sa dúyɛ́,　kʊ́lú nen tcįlekuyi
nɛlį.　ʔɛyit'á na dúyé-híle-lɛsą́.　nen
bɛk'éniyɛ nįgaɬ.　ʔɛkʊ́· si nɛk'éniyɛ tusą̂·
ʔɛt'axą ʔɛtθén ɬɛyą́nįɬθer-dɛ́ ʔɛyɛr nɛyą
níni·ya-ɣwalí,　héni.

dɛne nųniyɛ ʔɛnadlíi bɛɣą honi

Ս᠊ᗞ ᴗ᠄ᓂᒉ "ᐁᓇ᠌ᓐ ᐴᏀᔆ ᐦᐁᔆ

François Mandeville, transcribed by Li Fang-kuei

[PROLOGUE]

ʔįɫ̨ą́ɣį̨ dɛne ʔɛdɛɫkali húlyɛ.

ʔɛyi dɛne nųniyɛ hɛnadlí
sni.

ʔɛyi nųniyɛ ɣįlɛ́-tɬ'ą́ɣą
dɛne hɛnaθdlį-dɛ́
tcilekuyi lá ʔąt'ɛ ʔanat'į́
sni.

ta ʔoteyɛ́ hų́tɬ'ɛðɛ́ nį́únįɫθer hots'én dɛne ɣįlɛ́
sni.

ʔɛkúú ʔįɫá nųniyɛ naɣedlɛ́ɛ hoɣą holni.

[SCENE I]

ʔɛkúú ʔoteyɛ́ nį́únįɫθer nadlįú nųniyɛ ʔayɛɫni,

« ʔą́ɫų́ą́ nį́ hok'ɛ náɣwasθer yɛnį̨ðen-dɛ́
nuhwɛ-xɛ́ɫ nánanɛdðer.
ʔɛkwá ʔanɛdjá-dɛ́ yų́ųnaθɛ́ θá ɣį̨na-ixa,» yɛ́ɫni.

kúú ʔɛdɛɫkali,

« nųniyɛ naɣwasdlɛ́-híɫɛ yɛnį̨ðen.»

kúlú nųniyɛ ʔayɛ́ɫni,

« nųniyɛ hɛnaθį̨dlį-híɫɛ-dɛ́
nɛðiyɛ́-ixa θá-híɫɛ,» yɛ́ɫni.

THE STORY OF THE MAN WHO BECAME A WOLF

ᒍ ᐣᑐᑎ ᐅᑊ ᒍ ᒪᐣ ᑊᐅ ᐱᑳᑦ ᐊ ᐅᐧᔅᑊ

François Mandeville, translated by Ron Scollon

[PROLOGUE]

There was a man called Spread Wings.

From time to time he became a wolf.
This is what they say.

After he has been a wolf,
when he becomes a man again,
he becomes a young man.
This is what they say.

Three times he has lived to be an old man.
This is what they say.

This is the story he told about becoming a wolf again.

[SCENE I]

When he was very old, a wolf spoke to him,

"If you wish to live longer on the earth,
you must live with us again.
If you do that, you will live for a long time."

Spread Wings thought,

"I won't be a wolf again."

But the wolf said,

"If you don't become a wolf again,
you will die soon."

ʔɛdɛłkali ʔadi,

«ʔą́lų́ų́ nį́ hok'ɛ náɣwasθer yɛnɛsθen
ʔɛyit'á nų̨niyɛ ɣwasłé,» héni.

dɛdą̨né nų̨niyɛ hɛθɛlį̨.

kúú ʔɛyi t'ahi nų̨niyɛ yɛts'én yałtei-nį̨
nų̨niyɛ ts'éyą̨kuyi ʔɛyi
ʔadi-hik'ɛ́.

kúú ʔɛdɛłkali nų̨niyɛ hɛθɛlį̨ dɛdą̨né
nų̨niyɛ ts'éyą̨kuyi ʔayɛ́łni,

«sų̨naɣį̨,
yų̨ų̨tθɛ́ ʔɛtθén łą̨-lɛsą́.
dų̨hú ʔɛkozį́ huút'ás,» héni.

[SCENE II]

ʔɛkúú yų̨ų̨tθɛ́ hɛɛ́ð'az.

ʔɛyi nų̨niyɛ nį́únį̨łθer, kúlú náltła-hit'á
tu nɛtcá kúlú hóð'ą̨-híle yɛk'ɛ́ tθ'ánalguih.
ʔɛkwát'į̨-hį̨t'uú ʔɛts'į́naθɛ́ hozué-k'ɛ nį̨hį̨t'az.

ʔɛkúú ʔɛt'axą̨ ʔɛtθén-kɛɣɛ́ ʔahuuɣɛʔį̨.

betsų̨né ʔayɛ́łni,

«sų̨naɣį̨,
ʔɛkúú bér-ba hídðer.
diri bɛkɛɣɛ́ níl'į̨ ʔɛyi bér ʔą̨t'ɛ.

«ʔɛkúú si nį́únį̨łθer-hit'á sa dúyɛ́,
kúlú nen tcilekuyi nɛlį̨.
ʔɛyit'á na dúyɛ́-híle-lɛsą́.
nen bek'ɛ́niye nį̨gał.

«ʔɛkúú si nɛk'ɛ́niye tusáa

Spread Wings answered,

> "I want to live longer on the earth,
>   so I will become a wolf again."

He immediately became a wolf.

Then he realized that the wolf
who was speaking to him
was an old woman.

As soon as Spread Wings had become a wolf,
the old woman said to him,

> "Grandson,
>   there are probably many caribou up north.
>   Let's go that way."

[SCENE II]

They started north.

> Although the wolf was old, she went fast.
> So they came to the end of the big lake in no time.
> And doing so they finally came again to the barren ground.

Suddenly they saw caribou tracks.

His grandmother said,

> "Grandson,
>   we are hungry now.
>   These tracks we are seeing were left by meat.

> "I am old, and so it is impossible for me,
>   but you are a young man.
>   It is not impossible for you.
>   You go after it.

> "I'll start after you.

ʔɛtʼaxą ʔɛtθén ɬɛɣ́ánįɬθer-dɛ́
ʔɛyɛr nɛɣą níniiya-ɣwalí, » héni.

ʔɛkúú ʔɛdɛɬkali ʔɛtθén-kʼɛ́niyɛ tɛ́ðya.

hozuɛ́-kʼɛ níhįnįʔaz-nį
kúlú ʔąɬųą́ ʔąɬkʼɛ́ dɛtcin-yaze dárɛ́ðla.
ʔɛyi-ta ʔɛtθén heɬkáɬ.

tɛðɛ ʔɛldzinɛ́ nįðá ʔɛtθén nį́niɬkʼɛ hozuɛ́-kʼɛ ...

*If you kill a caribou,
I will come to you."*

Spread Wings started after the caribou.

*They came to the barren ground,
but there were still small pockets of woods.
He tracked the caribou among them.*

He tracked a long way in the moonlight on the barren ground ...

ᑌᓀ ᓄᐢᓂᔭ ᐦᐁᓇᐟᔒ ᐯᓚᐢ ᑊᐅᓂ

ᐯᑕᐢᐣᐊᐧ ᒪᐢᑌᐱᔅ

[PROLOGUE]

ᐦᐃᐢᑦᒍᐢᒋᐢ ᑌᓀ ᐦᐁᑌᔅᑲᔑ ᑊᐅᔭ.

ᐦᐁᔪ ᑌᓀ ᓄᐢᓂᔭ ᑊᐁᓇᐟᔑ
ᐁᐣᓂ.

ᐦᐁᔪ ᓄᐢᓂᔭ ᒋᐢᑐ-ᐟᒍᐢᓚᐢ
ᑌᓀ ᑊᐁᓇᐦᐟᔑᐢ-ᑌ
ᗰᑐᑯᒋ ᒍᐦᐊᐢᑌᑊ ᐦᐊᓇᑎᑊᐢ
ᐁᐣᓂ.

ᕦ ᐦᐅᗯᔭ ᑊᐅᐢᐟᑐᒣ ᓂᐢᐅᓂᐢᔅᒣᐟ ᑊᐅᐟᔪᐤ ᑌᓀ ᒋᐢᔑ
ᐁᐣᓂ.

ᐦᐁᑯ ᐦᐃᐢᑦᒍ ᓄᐢᓂᔭ ᓇᓚᐟᑐᐧ ᑊᐅᓚᐢ ᑊᐅᔅᓂ.

[SCENE I]

ᐦᐁᑯ ᐦᐅᗯᔭ ᓂᐢᐅᓂᐢᔅᒣᐟ ᓇᐟᔑᐢᐅ ᓄᐢᓂᔭ ᐦᐊᔭᔅᓂ.

ᐦᐊᐢᑦᓴᐢ ᓂᐢ ᑊᐅᑫᑊ ᓇᙆᐊᐧᐣᒣᐟ ᔭᓂᐢᒣᐤ-ᑌ
ᓄᙆᑊᐁ··-ᓚᔅ ᓇᓇᓀᐟᒣᐟ.
ᐦᐁᑲᐧᐦᐊᓀᐟᕮ-ᑌ ᔪᐢᓇᒣ ᒐ ᒋᐢᓇ-ᐃᓚ, ᔭᔅᓂ.

ᑯ ᐦᐁᑌᔅᑲᔑ,

ᓄᐢᓂᔭ ᓇᙆᐊᐧᐣᐟᑐ-ᑊᐃᑐ ᔭᓂᐢᒣᐤ.

ᑯᓴ ᓄᐢᓂᔭ ᐦᐊᔭᔅᓄ,

ᓄᐢᓂᔭ ᑊᐁᓇᒥᐢᐟᔑᐢ-ᑊᐃᑐ-ᑌ
ᓀᒥᔭ-ᐃᓚ ᒐ-ᑊᐃᑐ, ᔭᔅᓂ.

ᐦᐁᑌᔅᑲᔑ ᐦᐊᑎ,

″ᐊᐠᑦᔕᐠ ᓂᐠ ᑊᐅᑫᑊ ᓇᙆᐊᐧᐢᒉᐟ ᔦᓀᐢᒉᐣ
″ᐁᔨᑕᑊ ᓄᐠᓂᔦ-ᙆᐊᐧᐢᑦᑗ, ᑊᐁᓂ.

ᑌᑕᐠᓀ ᓄᐠᓂᔦ ᑊᐁᒉᒍᐠ.

ᑯ ″ᐁᔨ ᑕᐦᐃ ᓄᐠᓂᔦ ᔦᐟᓭᐣ ᔭᔆᙨᐃ-ᓂᐠ
ᓄᐠᓂᔦ ᐟᓭᔭᐠᑯᔨ ″ᐁᔨ
″ᐊᑎ-ᑊᐃᑫᑊ.

ᑯ ″ᐁᑌᔆᑲᒍ ᓄᐠᓂᔦ ᑊᐁᒉᒍᐠ ᑌᑕᐠᓀ
ᓄᐠᓂᔦ ᐟᓭᔭᑯᔨ ″ᐊᔦᔆᓂ,

ᓩᐠᓇᔑ,
ᔪᐠᐟᒉᐠ ″ᐁᐟᒉᐣ ᑦᓩᐠ-ᑗᓭ.
ᑐᐠᑊᐅ ″ᐁᑯᓇᐠ ᑊᐅᑕᑊᐢ, ᑊᐁᓂ.

[SCENE II]

″ᐁᑯ ᔪᐠᐟᒉᐠ ᑊᐁʰ″ᐊᐢ.

″ᐁᔨ ᓄᐠᓂᔦ ᓂᐠᐅᓂᐠᔆᒉᐟ, ᑯᔭ ᓇᔆᐟᓩ-ᑊᐃᑕᑊ
ᑕ ᓀᗴ ᑯᔭ ᑊᐅʰ″ᐊᐠ-ᑊᐃᑗ ᔦᑫᑊ ᕮᓇᔆᑯᐃᙆ.
″ᐁᑲᐧᑎᑊᐠ-ᑊᐃᑐᑊ ″ᐁᐟᓩᐠᓇᒉ ᑊᐅᕝᐁ-ᑫᑊ ᓂᐠᑊᐃᐠᑕᑊᐢ.

″ᐁᑯ ″ᐁᑕᑊᒑᐠ ″ᐁᐟᒉᐣ-ᑫᒑ ″ᐊᑊᐅᒑ″ᐃᐠ.

ᐯᐟᓩᐠᓀ ″ᐊᔦᔆᓂ,

ᓩᐠᓇᔑ,
″ᐁᑯ ᐯᐟ-ᐸ ᑊᐃᐟᒉᐟ.
ᑎᑎ ᐯᑫᑗ ᓂᔆ″ᐃᐠ ″ᐁᔨ ᐯᐟ ″ᐊᑌᑊ.

″ᐁᑯ ᓩ ᓂᐠᐅᓂᐠᔆᒉᐟ-ᑊᐃᑕᑊ ᓭ ᑐᔦ,
ᑯᔭ ᓀᐣ ᐟᙢᑗᑯᔨ ᓀᒍᐠ.
″ᐁᔨᑕᑊ ᓇ ᑐᔦ-ᑊᐃᑗ-ᑗᓭᐠ.
ᓀᐣ ᐯᑫᑖᓂᔦ ᓂᐠᑲᔆ.

″ᐁᑯ ᓩ ᓀᑫᑊᓂᔦ ᕮᓭ
″ᐁᑕᑊᑖᐠ ″ᐁᐟᒉᐣ ᑦᑗᑖᐠᓂᐠᔆᒉᐟ-ᑌ
″ᐁᔦᐟ ᓀᑖᐠ ᓂᓂᔭ-ᑖᐧᒍ, ᑊᐁᓂ.

"▽ᑯ "▽ᑌˢᑲᢒ "▽ᐧᒉᐧ-ᕿᑊᓂᒎ ᗙʰᐳ.

ᐧᗺᒐ▽-ᕿ ᓂᐧᒣᐃᐧᓂᐧᐧᐊᐣ-ᓂᐧ

ᑯᒐ "ᐊᐧᑢᐳ "ᐊᐧᔕᕿᐧ ᑌᐧᒪᐳ-ᐳᣵ ᑕᑌʰᘗ.

"▽ᔭ-Ꮸ "▽ᐧᒉᐳ ᐧ▽ˢᑲˢ.

ᗙᒉ "▽ˢᐧᐳᣠ ᓂᐧᒣ "▽ᐧᒉᐳ ᓂᐧᓂˢᕿᐧ ᐧᗺᒐ▽-ᕿᐧ ...

Bibliography

Bringhurst, Robert. 2004. *Prosodies of Meaning: Literary Form in Native North America.* The University of Manitoba 2002 Belcourt Lecture in Linguistics. Winnipeg: Voices of Rupert's Land.

———. 2006. *The Tree of Meaning.* Kentville, N.S.: Gaspereau Press; Berkeley: Counterpoint.

———. 2008. *The Surface of Meaning: Books and Book Design in Canada.* Vancouver: CCSP Press.

Darnell, Regna. 1974. "Correlates of Cree Narrative Performance. " Pp 315–336 in Richard Bauman and Joel Sherzer (eds.). *Explorations in the Ethnography of Speaking.* New York: Cambridge University Press.

Dauenhauer, Nora Marks, and Richard Dauenhauer (eds.). 1987. *Haa Shuká, Our Ancestors: Tlingit Oral Narratives.* Seattle and London: University of Washington Press; Juneau: Sealaska Heritage Foundation.

———. 1990. *Haa Tuwunáagu Yís, for Healing Our Spirit: Tlingit Oratory.* Seattle & London: University of Washington Press; Juneau: Sealaska Heritage Foundation.

———. 1994. *Haa Kusteeyí, Our Culture: Tlingit Life Stories.* Seattle & London: University of Washington Press; Juneau: Sealaska Heritage Foundation.

Dauenhauer, Richard. 1974. Text and Context of Tlingit Oral tradition. Unpublished Ph.D. dissertation, University of Wisconsin, Madison.

———. 1975. "The Narrative Frame: Style and Personality in Tlingit Prose Narrative." Pp 65–81 in Stephen Mannenbach (ed.). *Folklore Forum,* Special Issue: *Trends and New Vistas in Contemporary Native American Folklore Study.* Indiana University Bibliographic and Special Series, 15.9. Bloomington, Ind.: Folklore and Ethnomusicology Publications.

Hymes, Dell. 1976. "Louis Simpson's 'The Deserted Boy'." *Poetics* 5(2), 119–155.

———. 1977. "Discovering Oral Performance and Measured Verse in American Indian Narrative." *New Literary History* 8: 431–457.

———. 1981. *'In vain I tried to tell you': Essays in Native American Ethnopoetics.* Philadelphia: University of Pennsylvania Press.

Hymes, Virginia. 1987. "Warm Springs Sahaptin Narrative Analysis." Pp 62–102 in Joel Sherzer and Anthony C. Woodbury (eds.). *Native American Discourse: Poetics and Rhetoric.* Cambridge and New York: Cambridge University Press.

Jacobs, Melville. 1959. *Content and Style of an Oral Literature.* Chicago: University of Chicago Press.

Li Fang-kuei. [1928]. Chipewyan texts and field notes. Fanggui Li Collection, Ms. Coll. 119, American Philosophical Society Library, Philadelphia.

————. 1933a. "Chipewyan Consonants." *Bulletin of the Institute of History and Philology of the Academia Sinica* (Supplementary Volume 1): 429–467.

————. 1933b. "A List of Chipewyan Stems." *International Journal of American Linguistics* 7(3–4): 122–151.

————. 1946. "Chipewyan." In Harry Hoijer (ed.). *Linguistic Structures of Native America*. Viking Fund Publications in Anthropology, No. 6. New York: Viking Fund.

————. 1964. "A Chipewyan Ethnological Text." *International Journal of American Linguistics* 30(2): 132–136.

Li Fang-kuei and Ronald Scollon. 1976. *Chipewyan Texts*. Taipei: Academia Sinica.

Scollon, Ron. 1976. "The Framing of Chipewyan Narratives in Performance: Titles, Initials and Finals." *Working Papers in Linguistics,* Department of Linguistics, University of Hawai'i, 7(4): 97–107.

————. 1977. "Two Discourse Markers in Chipewyan Narratives." *International Journal of American Linguistics* 43(1): 60–64.

————. 1979a. "Variable Data and Linguistic Convergence: Texts and Contexts in Chipewyan." *Language in Society* 8(2): 223–242.

————. 1979b. "236 years of Variability in Chipewyan Consonants." *International Journal of American Linguistics* 45(4): 332–342.

————. 1985. "The Sequencing of Clauses in Chipewyan Narratives." Pp 113–131 in Johanna Nichols and Anthony C. Woodbury (eds.). *Grammar Inside and Outside the Clause*. New York: Cambridge University Press.

Scollon, Ron, and Suzanne B. K. Scollon. 1979. *Linguistic Convergence: An Ethnography of Speaking at Fort Chipewyan, Alberta*. New York: Academic Press.

————. 1981. *Narrative, Literacy and Face in Interethnic Communication*. Norwood, N.J.: Ablex.

————. 1984. "Cooking It Up and Boiling It Down: Abstracts in Athabaskan Children's Story Retellings." Pp 173–197 in Deborah Tannen (ed.). *Coherence in Spoken and Written Discourse*. Norwood, N.J.: Ablex.

————. 1989. "Obituary: Fang Kuei Li (1902–1987)." *American Anthropologist* 91(4): 1008–1009.

Tedlock, Dennis. 1972a. *Finding the Center: Narrative Poetry of the Zuni Indians*. New York: Dial [2nd ed., *Finding the Center: The Art of the Zuni Storyteller*. Lincoln: University of Nebraska Press, 1999].

————. 1972b. "On the Translation of Style in Oral Narrative." Pp 114–133 in Américo Paredes and Richard Bauman (eds.). *Toward New Perspectives in Folklore*. Austin: University of Texas Press.

Toelken, Barre. 1969. "The 'Pretty Language' of Yellowman: Genre, Mode, and Texture in Navaho Coyote Narratives." *Genre* 2(3): 211–235.

Yue-Hashimoto, Anne. 2000/2001. "Professor Li Fang-kuei: A Personal Memoir." *Asia Notes* (Newsletter of the Department of Asian Languages and Literature, University of Washington, Seattle), 4(1): 5–6.